THE WORLD'S GREATEST SHOWMAN

The Life of P. T. Barnum

THE
WORLD'S GREATEST
SHOWMAN

THE LIFE OF P. T. BARNUM

──────── ★ ────────

by **J. BRYAN, III.**

Landmark BOOKS

RANDOM HOUSE · NEW YORK

ACKNOWLEDGMENTS

Biographers of Barnum have at their disposal the enormous fund of his autobiography, *Struggles and Triumphs,* and I have levied heavy drafts on the version edited by George S. Bryan (2 vols., Alfred A. Knopf, 1927). Four other books I have also mined, but less freely. These are, in order of my indebtedness, *Barnum,* by M. R. Werner (Harcourt, Brace & Co., 1923), *Barnum Presents: General Tom Thumb,* by Alice Curtis Desmond (Macmillan, 1954), *The Unknown Barnum,* by Harvey W. Root (Harper & Bros., 1927) and *The Big Top,* by Fred Bradna and Hartzell Spence (Simon & Schuster, 1952).

It would be tedious to list the rest of my printed sources, but I wish to express my gratitude to the people who directed me toward them, or made them available, or otherwise assisted me. Foremost are Miss Elizabeth Sterling Seeley, curator of the Barnum Museum at Bridgeport, Connecticut, and Mr. Herbert French, of New York City, both of whom were tireless in providing information and in rescuing me from errors of ignorance and misjudgment. Mrs. Vivienne Mars, librarian in charge of the Harry Hertzberg Circus Collection at San Antonio, Texas, was similarly helpful. Mrs. Leonidas Westervelt of Great Neck, Long Island, opened to me her late husband's rich collection of Barnumana. Mr. Tom Parkinson of *Billboard* put me in touch with men who had known Barnum personally. And Mr. Maynard Morris made it possible for me to hear and take notes on the recording mentioned on page 169. I owe more than mere thanks to each of them, but I can—and do— pay them at least that much now.

The verses by Walter de la Mare on page 37 are from his *Ding Dong Bell,* published by Faber and Faber, 1936; and those on page 110 are from Vachel Lindsay's "Simon Legree," which appears in his *Collected Poems,* Copyright, 1917, 1945, by The Macmillan Company. Both extracts are quoted by permission of their publishers. The quotation from Stephen Vincent Benét on pages 4-5 is from the story "The Angel with the Yankee," which appeared in *The Last Circle,* Copyright, 1940, by Rosemary Carr Benét.

J. Bryan, III

Washington, D. C.,
February, 1956.

To
Henry Ringling North,
my first guide to the wonderland
of the "back yard,"
and to
Buddy,
in affectionate memory of
Chief Thunder Wolf,
Chief Crazy Wolf and
Chief Irving Wolf.

Contents

THE WORLD'S GREATEST SHOWMAN
The Life of P. T. Barnum

A Connecticut Yankee

P. T. BARNUM WAS A BIG, BLUFF, BRAWNY MAN WITH curly hair and a potato-like nose, and a dimple in his chin and a spark in his eye. He seemed larger than life, and gaudier, like one of his own circus posters, and only circus superlatives seemed fit to describe him: GRANDEST, RAREST, UNIQUE, MOST STUPENDOUS. He was a nonesuch—nobody like him before, nobody like him since.

He prided himself on having "amused and instructed more persons than any other manager that ever lived." People called him "a super-magnified Santa Claus." More of them *paid* to enter his museum than entered the British Museum free of charge. He was the world's greatest showman and one of the most famous Americans in the world. Six generations of Connecticut

Yankees stood behind him; he was Connecticut born and bred, and Yankee from twang to trickery; yet hardly a king or queen in Europe had not made him welcome.

When his home town elected him mayor in 1875, somebody said, "The whole civilized world knows that Barnum is Mayor of Bridgeport, but seven-eighths of them couldn't tell you where it is or how to spell it." They didn't need to. His letters wanted no more address than

P. T. Barnum
America

His name is written large on his land—at Barnum, Iowa, Barnum, Minnesota, Barnum, Texas, Barnum, West Virginia, Barnum, Wisconsin, and Barnumton, Missouri. Some of his "humbugs," such as

THIS WAY TO THE EGRESS

belong to American folklore; and whether or not he actually fathered "A sucker is born every minute," no list of Americanism is complete without it.

Stephen Vincent Benét wrote that America is "an outsize country and it likes outsize things. It even likes being fooled in an outsize way. And that's what Barnum knew. He fooled them but he gave them their money's worth—he gave people things they'd remember the rest of their lives. . . ." Not the least was himself.

New York City was still the village of Nieuw Amsterdam when, around 1655, young Thomas Barnham landed there from England—the first of his line in America. Nothing survives to explain why the twelve-year-old boy left his father and mother and ventured alone to the wild land across the ocean. The records say only that a farmer from Norwalk, Connecticut, guaranteed his passage, and that he soon worked it off; and then they fall silent until 1685, when he appears again, as one of the first settlers of Danbury. He died there ten years later, leaving five sons and five daughters. They themselves were so fruitful that within a century the twenty-three Barnums (as they now spelled it) on the Danbury tax-list were outnumbered only by the thirty Benedicts.

The Barnums ran to stern old Bible names: Ezra, Nathaniel, Eben, Noah, Ira, Abel, Ephraim. Ephraim, a captain of militia in the Revolutionary War, had a son named Philo, who was a Jack-of-all-trades, successful at none. However, the family fertility was still strong in him. Like Thomas, his great-great-grandfather, he had ten children. The sixth, a son, was born at Bethel, a few miles from Danbury, on July 5, 1810. (Since he grew up to represent the typical American in the portrait gallery of nations, he should—ideally—

have been born a day earlier, on the national birth-day.) His mother had him christened after her father, Phineas Taylor. A more fitting name for one of the greatest self-advertisers in history could not have been found. "Phineas" means "mouth of brass."

Grandpa Taylor was the ancestor of young "Tale," as the family called the boy, in more ways than one. The old man had a county-wide reputation as a justice of the peace, but his reputation as a prankster was almost state-wide. Tale once said of him, "He would go farther, wait longer, work harder, and contrive deeper to carry out a practical joke, than for anything else under heaven." In evidence, there was the story of his trip down to New York, in a party of fourteen Danbury men. The last leg, from Norwalk by water, should have taken only overnight, but their sloop was becalmed for three days, and Mr. Taylor had the only razor aboard. He agreed to lend it to the others—in-cluding a clergyman with a full red beard—provided that each, in fairness to all, shave only one cheek, then pass the razor to his neighbor. Not until all were half shaven would the first man shave his other cheek. Mr. Taylor led off. When the turn came back to him, he shaved himself clean, and then, while stropping the razor for the next man, "accidentally" dropped it over-board. . . .

Bethel was still almost a frontier community in those days. Indian attacks were still fresh in the minds of many of the townsfolk, and Tale's uncles and aunts often told him about the burning of Danbury by the British in 1777. That wasn't so far back. In 1815, the old-timers still wore knee-breeches. Suicides were still buried at a crossroads, and there was still a public whipping post. Droves of hogs roved the streets. People wore homespun, and their standard diet was beans, rye bread, applesauce, corned beef, salt pork, and hasty pudding. For drink, there was rum, and a cider mixture called "gumption."

Tale wrote in his autobiography, *Struggles and Triumphs:* "Like most farmers' boys, I was obliged to drive and fetch the cows, carry in firewood, shell corn, weed beets and cabbages, and in due time handled the shovel and the hoe—but I never really liked to work . . . the farm was no place for me. Hand work was decidedly not in my line." On the other hand, "Head work I was excessively fond of. I was always ready to concoct fun or lay plans for money-making."

Or even to study. Tale stood near the top of his class at school. He was especially good at arithmetic. His teacher boasted about him to a neighbor and routed him out of bed in the middle of the night and set him a hard sum. Tale did it, too, quickly and correctly.

Years later, he returned to Bethel to dedicate a fountain he had given. "I can distinctly remember events which occurred when I was four years old," he said in his speech. "I remember seeing my father and our neighbors put through military drill every day in

1814 for the war with Great Britain." Even more memorable was 1816, "the year without a summer," also known as "eighteen hundred and starve to death." Bethel had frost, ice and snow in June, frost and ice in July, and half an inch of ice in August. The next year, when Tale was seven, he saw a public hanging. When he was eleven, he spent "the happiest two hours of my life" at his first circus. The other high spot of his youth was in 1822, when a drover passed through town with a herd of cattle bound for New York City and hired Tale as an assistant.

When he got to New York, he did what any other boy would have done: he went sightseeing, spent all his money on a cap pistol, a knife and "torpedoes," and then exchanged them for molasses candy. Back home, when his mother examined his wardrobe and found two pocket handkerchiefs and one pair of stockings missing, she whipped him and sent him to bed.

But presently, Tale's money began to stick to his fingers. He owned a calf and a sheep. He built up his cash capital by selling cherry rum and "cookania," a kind of candy. His grandfather paid him ten cents a day to ride a lead horse before a team of plough oxen. He would have banked a nice little stake, if he hadn't had to buy his own clothes, thanks to his father's thriftlessness. Worse, Philo Barnum was borrowing right and left, and when he died in 1825, he was so badly in debt that his estate could pay only fifty cents on the dollar. Tale's savings went into the pot; he had to get trusted for the shoes he wore to the funeral. He used to say, "I literally began the world with nothing and was barefooted at that."

The next three years, Tale tried job after job. He clerked in a local store for six dollars a month and board, then clerked in Brooklyn, then moved over to Manhattan and ran a "porterhouse" (a tavern), caught smallpox, returned to Bethel, then returned to New York. Finally, in 1828, he went back to Bethel again and opened a store in Grandpa Taylor's carriage shed, selling fruit, oysters, ale and confectionery.

"There are some persons," he wrote, "so constituted that they can never be satisfied to labor for a fixed salary, let it be ever so great. I am one of that sort. . . . This beginning of business on my own account was an eventful era in my life."

He spent $50 fixing up the shed and $70 on stock. His first day of business he took in $63, which so impressed him that he laid in a side line of pocketbooks, combs, beads, rings, knives and toys. One of his next customers, a young man, picked out a pocketbook and asked for credit. Taylor told him that "if he wanted to buy any article of necessity, I should not object to trust him for a short time, but it struck me that a pocketbook was a decided superfluity for a man who had no money."

Within the year he branched out into another side line, one which presently became his main source of income: lottery tickets. They were legal in those days, and Taylor made a handsome profit from them. For a while, he considered moving to Tennessee and opening a lottery business there, but he finally decided against it. One factor in his decision was a certain fair, rosy, buxom girl with beautiful white teeth. She was Charity Hallett, a "tailoress" or dressmaker. They had met during his first clerkship, early in 1826, and he had been courting her ever since.

In the fall of 1829 "Chairy," as he called her, skipped off to New York, and he followed her and married her. His mother thought Taylor could have done better than the tailoress, but hers was a minority opinion. Taylor himself recorded that the rest of the townsfolk considered Charity Hallett "altogether too good" for him. They lived in perfect happiness until her death forty-four years later.

The young couple—he was nineteen, she twenty-one—returned to Bethel soon after the wedding. Taylor built them a house (it is still standing) and tried auctioning some books he had bought in New York, but they were stolen. He celebrated his coming-of-age in July, 1831 by opening a new store. Sales were often slow, but discussions—especially of religious and political questions—were always fast, and in many of them Taylor found material for letters to the *Danbury Recorder*. Some the editor refused to publish. Taylor rejected his explanation that they were too controversial, and hot-headedly started a newspaper of his own, *The Herald of Freedom,* so that he would no longer be subject to timidities. The vigor and boldness of the *Herald's* pages resulted in a succession of libel suits. One of them, brought by a deacon whom Taylor had accused in print of "taking usury of an orphan boy," got the young editor a fine of $100 and a sentence of sixty days in jail.

According to *History of Danbury, Connecticut,* Taylor was not in the least daunted. On the contrary, he had a good room, lived well, and edited his paper as usual, between visits from his friends. The sixty days ended with a testimonial banquet, after which—to cheers, band music and cannon salutes—he rode home proudly in a coach drawn by six horses.

But the newspaper business, like too many others, was not for him. Restless and irresolute, he sold both his press and his store. He might have stayed to develop his lottery connections, but by that time lotteries had been declared illegal, and now there was nothing to hold him in Bethel. In November, 1834, he and Chairy, with their year-old daughter, Caroline Cornelia, headed for the larger, greener pastures of New York. He never lived in Bethel again.

The Beginning of Humbug

THE WINTER OF 1834-35 WAS A HARD ONE. BUSINESS was bad, little Caroline's health was poor, and the only job Taylor could find in New York was selling caps on commission. The following spring, however, several debts owed him from Bethel were suddenly repaid, and with this windfall he opened a boarding house at 52 Frankfort Street, near the steamboat landing. He also bought an interest in a grocery store. Both businesses prospered, but neither seemed to satisfy a longing of his so strange and vague that he could hardly identify it. And then, on a summer day, into the boarding house walked his fate, in the person of one Coley Bartram, of Redding, Connecticut. It was the pivot moment of Barnum's career.

Bartram showed him an advertisement in *The Penn-*

sylvania Inquirer announcing the exhibition, in the Philadelphia Masonic Hall, of "Joice Heth, a negress aged 161 years, who formerly belonged to the father of Gen. Washington." The notice continued, "All who have seen this extraordinary woman are satisfied of the truth of the account of her age. . . . The original bill of sale of Augustine Washington, in his own handwriting, and other evidence which the proprietor has in his possession, will satisfy even the most incredulous."

Bartram said that he and R. W. Lindsay, of Kentucky, had been joint owners of Joice Heth. Bartram had sold out, and now Lindsay too wanted to sell and retire.

Barnum left for Philadelphia at once. Here is his own account of what he saw:

The old woman might almost as well have been called a thousand years old. She was apparently in good health and spirits, but although she could move one of her arms at will, her lower limbs could not be straightened. She was totally blind, and her eyes were so deeply sunken that the eyeballs seemed to have disappeared altogether. She had no teeth, but possessed a head of thick, bushy gray hair. The fingers of her left hand were drawn down so as nearly to close it. The nails were about four inches in length, and extended above her wrist. The nails upon her large toes also had grown to the thickness of nearly a quarter of an inch.

Joice swore she had been present when "dear little George" was born. She was the first person to dress him. "In fact," she liked to say, "I raised him."

When Lindsay produced a bill of sale dated February 5, 1727, for "one negro woman, named Joice Heth, aged fifty-four years," Barnum was convinced. Lindsay asked $3,000, but Barnum shaved the price to $1,000. He had half the sum; the other half he borrowed, and presently the old woman was his. He took her to New York and put her on exhibition at Niblo's Garden, in a room lent him by William Niblo in return for half the gross receipts.

Opening day, the day of P. T. Barnum's debut as a showman, was August 10, 1835. It is one of the most important days in the history of show business—not only a red-letter day, but a brass-band day, a sawdust-and-spangles day, a day of lions and elephants, clowns and canvas, whistles and banners, peanuts, popcorn and pink lemonade. It is American Circusdom's Glorious Fourth of July.

Old Joice pulled in a steady $1,500 a week for several weeks, so Barnum soon paid off his investment and laid by a nest egg. When the stream of New Yorkers began to dwindle, he took her on a tour of New England. Boston was their most memorable stop, for two reasons. First, Barnum, who dearly loved a pun, read in a local newspaper, "It *rejoice-heth* us exceedingly to know that we shall be permitted to look upon the old patriarch." Second, he discovered that attendance could be stimulated by controversy. When Boston audiences too began to dwindle, he sent one of the newspapers an anonymous letter complaining that Joice was "a humbug" (one of his favorite words)—nothing but an automaton constructed of whalebone, springs and rubber. People who had never seen her now had their curiosity whetted, while others became impatient for a second look, to learn whether they had been deceived. "The consequence was," Barnum wrote smugly, "our audience again largely increased."

In Philadelphia a few months later, he exploited the false controversy again. By then he had turned Joice over to an associate, Levi Lyman, while he himself conducted the tour of Signor Vivalla, a juggler. Vivalla had happened to be playing Albany "day and date"—in the circus phrase—with Joice, and Barnum had been so impressed by his dexterity that he had engaged him for one year, for $12 a week and expenses.

Vivalla's repertory included balancing muskets on his nose, spinning plates, and stalking across the stage on ten-foot stilts. He spoke fluent English, but Barnum forbade him to do so and introduced the stunts himself —a role he considered so important that it required italics in his autobiography: *"This was my 'first appearance on any stage.'"*

From Albany, he took Vivalla to New York, Boston and Washington. Snowstorms cut attendance in Washington; Barnum had to pawn his watch and chain for two fares to Philadelphia. The bad weather continued there, but a rival juggler, one Robert, obligingly became party to a "grudge match" for a thousand-dollar forfeit, and Barnum ended by clearing several hundred dollars.

Meanwhile, old Joice had become too feeble for further travel, so Barnum retired her to Bethel. When she died there in February 1836, he had the body driven to New York in a sleigh, and sent for a surgeon who had asked to perform the post mortem. Other physicians, and editors and clergymen, also came. The first few incisions, laying bare the arteries around the heart, proved that Joice, far from being 161, was scarcely half that age.

Next day's *Sun* carried the story under the headline,

PRECIOUS HUMBUG EXPOSED

Levi Lyman thereupon called on the editor of the *Herald*, James Gordon Bennett, and managed to convince him that the body was not that of Joice Heth at all, but of "a respectable old negress called Aunt Nelly," from Harlem. Joice herself was alive, in Connecticut, Lyman said. As fast as he poured this nonsense out, Bennett soaked it up. Printed, it drew jeers and ridicule, of course, and Bennett confronted Lyman angrily. Lyman admitted the "harmless joke" and now, as a recompense, promised to tell the *real* story for the first time. And *again* the gullible Bennett printed column after column of free advertising for Barnum, including statements that he had discovered Joice on a Kentucky plantation, had had all her teeth extracted, and had schooled her in the details of the Washington family.

Barnum took no part. It was already his policy to confirm or deny nothing. He was well aware that wherever such controversies turned, they served a showman's purpose by keeping his name before the public.

Did Barnum know that he was sponsoring a "humbug"? Was he aware that Joice was not nearly so old as he was representing her? Many years later, he wrote of the original joint owner, Lindsay:

I never had anything to do with him except to buy from him in perfect good faith an old *negress,* which he falsely represented as the "Nurse of Washington" and which he imposed on me as such, by aid of a *forged Bill of Sale* purporting to have been made by the *father* of George Washington. I honestly *believed* all this. . . .

Perhaps he did, but he cannot silence the skeptic's whisper. There is scarcely an early chapter in his autobiography that is not peppered with anecdotes of what he approvingly calls "Yankee tricks" or "Yankee cuteness," but what someone less indulgent would call downright dishonesty. His native Connecticut earned its nickname, "The Nutmeg State," by the local practice of selling "nutmegs" carved of cedarwood. Barnum wrote of his own storekeeping days:

Many of our customers were hatters, and we took hats in payment for goods. There is probably no trade in which there can be more cheating than in hats. The best fur was

otter, the poorest was cony [rabbit]. The hatters mixed
their inferior furs with a little of their best, and sold us the
hats for "otter." We in turn mixed our sugars, teas, and
liquors, and gave them the most valuable names. The customers cheated us in their fabrics; we cheated the customers with our goods. Each party expected to be cheated, if
it were possible. Our ground coffee was as good as burned
peas, beans, and corn could make.

Throughout his book, Barnum's loudest applause
goes to the skillful dissembler and deceiver, the practical joker, the sharp trader, the man who "puts something over" on someone else. Therefore when he says
of Joice Heth's masquerade, "I honestly *believed* all
this," the chances are it was simply an extension of his
deceit, a final flight of the humbug.

His business motto was, "Let the buyer beware!"
He would never cheat to the extent of theft, or of re-
neging on a bargain. But it must be remembered that in
the 1830s Yankees made a distinction between dishonesty and misrepresentation. The former was a punish-
able offense, of course; but the latter, if successful, was
considered admirable. It must also be remembered that
Barnum was deeply religious. If he had considered his
humbugs as sin, rather than as clever, amusing frauds,
he would never have offered them to the public.

As a final note on Joice Heth, her remains were
buried at Barnum's expense in the village cemetery at
Bethel.

Barnum Buys a Museum

THE FIVE YEARS THAT FOLLOWED 1836—THE YEARS
that carried Barnum from twenty-six to thirty-one
years of age—were a hotchpotch of fruitless labor, aim-
less travel and roguish adventure. He blacked his face
and sang Negro songs in South Carolina. He was
threatened with a pistol in Ohio. He bought a river
steamer in Mississippi. He was thrown into jail in
Pennsylvania. He preached a sermon in Massachusetts.
He narrowly missed being tarred, feathered and ridden
on a rail in Maryland. He formed and dissolved half a
dozen partnerships in half a dozen enterprises. He
owned an itinerant circus, "Barnum's Grand Scientific
and Musical Theater," managed a dancer, wrote articles and advertisements, traded in sugar and molasses,
peddled *Sears' Pictorial Illustrations of the Bible,* and
manufactured cologne and shoe blacking.

Withal, 1841 found him "at the very bottom round of fortune's ladder. I had now arrived at an age when it was necessary to make one grand effort to raise myself above want and to think soberly of laying up something for 'a rainy day'. My recent enterprises had not been productive . . . my funds were decidedly low. My family [which now included a second daughter, Helen Maria, born in 1840] was in poor health."

So he bought a museum! Scudder's American Museum was its full name, and it stood at the corner of Broadway and Ann Street, in the heart of New York City. St. Paul's Church faced the entrance. The best hotel in town, the Astor House, was across the street. Trinity Church and City Hall Park were near by. The best restaurant, Delmonico's, was four blocks away. The two largest newspapers, the *Tribune* and the *Herald,* were published in the neighborhood.

The Museum's reputation was as good as its location. It had been founded in 1810, and $50,000 had been spent in building up a collection of curiosities so immense that no visitor could exhaust it in a single day. Scudder himself had recently died, and his daughters were eager to sell out, since neither they nor their trustees knew anything about the museum business. The asking price of $15,000 was reasonable, and Barnum would have struck the bargain at once, except that he didn't have $15,000 or even $1,500. Yet he was determined to buy. A friend asked him incredulously, *"You* buy the American Museum? What do you intend buying it with?"

"Brass," said Barnum, "for silver and gold have I none."

The five-story building that housed the collection was owned by a retired merchant, Francis W. Olmsted. Barnum wrote him, announcing his hopes and confessing his poverty, and proposing that Mr. Olmsted buy the collection, pay Barnum $12.50 a week to manage it, and retain all income above this until the cost and the rent ($2,500 a year) were completely discharged, at which time the collection would be Barnum's.

"You may bind me in any way," his letter continued, "and as tightly as you please—only give me a chance to dig out, or scratch out, and I will either do so or forfeit all the labor and trouble which I may have incurred."

Finally, he said, such an arrangement would secure a permanent tenant for the building, whereas it would probably lose under any other arrangement, since the Museum was threatened with failure.

Olmsted sent for him. Barnum recited his experience and qualifications, and presented a list of showmen and newspapermen who would testify to his character. Their second interview opened with Olmsted's abrupt, "Mr. Barnum, I don't like your references!"

Barnum stammered, "I—I regret to hear it, sir."

Olmsted began to laugh. "They all speak *too* well of you! In fact, they all talk as if they were partners of yours and intended to share the profit."

Olmsted then said that he was prepared to accept Barnum's proposal under the following additional terms:

1. Olmsted would appoint a ticket-taker and accountant who would render a weekly statement;

2. Barnum and his family would take an apartment in an adjoining building, at an additional rent of $500 a year;

3. Barnum would sign a five-year lease;

4. Barnum would post a piece of unencumbered real estate as extra security.

This last condition was a stumper. Barnum owned several small tracts around Bethel, but they were already top-heavy with mortgages. What to do? Suddenly, he thought of Ivy Island. . . .

Turn back to 1810 and to Phineas Taylor. Because Tale was not only his first grandchild but his namesake as well, old Phineas gave him as a birth-present the deed to Ivy Island, a tract near Bethel village. Barnum said that from the year he was born, scarcely a week passed without his grandfather's gravely reminding all Bethel that ownership of Ivy Island, "the most valuable farm in Connecticut," made Taylor the richest child in town. His mother often referred to his "immense possessions," and the neighbors expressed surprise and gratitude that, despite his wealth, he would condescend to play with their children. And then, around his twelfth birthday, he persuaded his father to let the hired man take him to see his "precious patrimony."

His mother's farewell words were, "Don't become so excited when you see your property as to let your joy make you sick, and don't feel above speaking to your brothers and sisters when you return!"

He promised, and set out.

Ivy Island proved to be five acres of bog and thicket, buzzing with hornets, crawling with snakes and not worth a farthing—another of old Phineas Taylor's practical jokes. But his grandson had the last laugh. Nineteen years later, when Olmsted asked him for security, the vision of Ivy Island—"not in its painful reality, but in all the beauty in which my youthful imagination had pictured it—came dancing to my relief." He offered it, and Olmsted authorized him to open negotiations for the collection.

After some bargaining, Scudder's administrator, John Heath, reduced his price to $12,000, and Barnum took an option in Olmsted's name—only to be told, when he went to sign the deed a few days later, that Heath had meanwhile found another buyer, at $15,000, and had taken a $1,000 binder. Barnum protested, but Heath merely shrugged. Barnum and he had nothing in writing, he pointed out, and his first responsibility was to Scudder's orphan daughters.

The buyer was Peale's Museum Company, a syndicate of buccaneers whose prime intention, Barnum soon discovered, was to combine the two museums, issue new stock, cut a plump melon of dividends, and leave the public with the rind. Forthwith, Barnum began stuffing the local newspapers with articles tipping the plot. How effective they were became clear when the syndicate sent for him and invited him to manage the New York Museum, as the combination was to be called, at $3,000 a year, beginning January 1, 1842— a month away. Barnum accepted. As he was leaving, the syndicate's president remarked, "Of course, we shall have no more of your squibs through the newspapers?"

Barnum replied demurely, "I ever try to serve the interests of my employers."

His careful choice of words was inspired by a fact he had just learned from Heath: the syndicate had contracted to pay the $14,000 balance on December 26th, and in event of forfeit or delay, Heath would sell to Barnum promptly on the 27th. The syndicate ignored the 26th, as Barnum had hoped and surmised, and next morning he was back in show business. His first act was to send the following letter:

AMERICAN MUSEUM
New York
December 27, 1841.

To the President and Directors of the New York Museum:

Gentlemen:—It gives me great pleasure to inform you that you are placed upon the Free List of this establishment until further notice.

P. T. BARNUM, *Proprietor.*

Phineas Taylor Barnum. (*The Barnum Museum*)

"Iranistan," the first and most fantastic of Barnum's Bridge-port mansions. (*The Barnum Museum*)

The American Museum, on Broadway, made Barnum's fortune. Note that next door is Genin the Hatter, who paid a record $225 for a ticket to Jenny Lind's first American concert. (*Museum of the City of New York*)

left: His second, "Lindencroft," was named for Jenny Lind. (*The Barnum Museum*)

(Elizabeth Sterling Seeley)

Jenny Lind.

When General Tom Thumb married Lavinia Warren in 1863, it was a great day for Barnum too. (*The Barnum Museum*)

left: More than 30,000 people welcomed Jenny to New York in 1850. (*Courtesy of the New York Historical Society, New York City*)

Jumbo never carried nearly this many children at one time; Barnum's posters always exaggerated. (*The Strobridge Lithographing Co.*)

The American Museum was destroyed in 1865 by the second of Barnum's five great fires. (*Courtesy of the New York Historical Society, New York City*)

The carved doors of this elegant old circus wagon slid back to reveal the animal cages. (*New York Public Library*)

Today's elephant acts differ little from this early one of Barnum's. (*New York Public Library*)

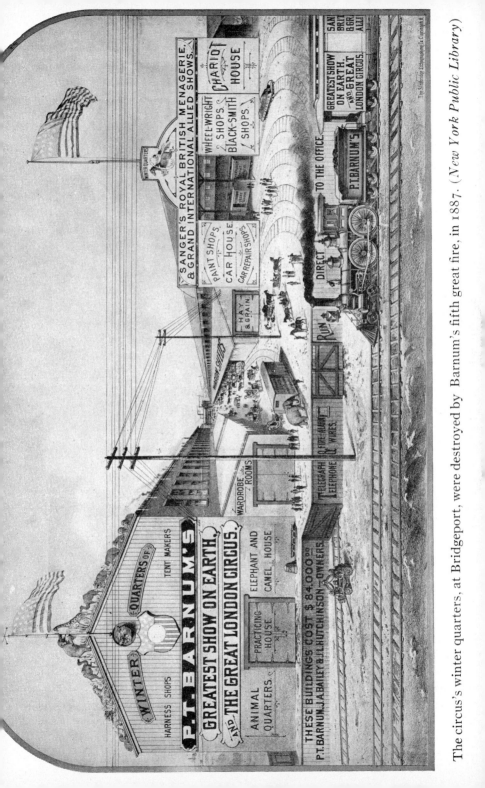

The circus's winter quarters, at Bridgeport, were destroyed by Barnum's fifth great fire, in 1887. (*New York Public Library*)

1890: The big red-and-gold band wagon leads a Barnum & Bailey parade. (*Courtesy Alfred J. Meyer*)

One of Barnum's famous stunts: An elephant and its keeper plowing a field beside the New York & New Haven tracks. (*The Barnum Museum*)

Two clowns, Chesty and Jo-jo, from the Ringling Brothers,
Barnum & Bailey troupe.

4

The "Fejee Mermaid"

THE AMERICAN MUSEUM OPENED UNDER ITS NEW MAN-
agement on New Year's Day, 1842. Barnum's ambi-
tion was to make it the talk of the town. To achieve
this, he figured that two things were essential: first, an
enormous and ever-changing variety of entertainment
on top of the permanent collection; and second, vigorous and constant publicity.

The permanent collection consisted of a gallery of
portraits of national figures, a Hall of Statuary, and a
small menagerie of animals both alive and stuffed.
Among the live animals were a boa constrictor, "The
Prince of Serpents," and an orang-outang, "The Wild
Man of the Woods." There were models of Paris, Je-
rusalem and Dublin. There was a mechanical man, and
a mechanical bird that flapped its wings. There were

panoramas and dioramas called "The Creation," "The Deluge," "A Fairy Grotto" and "A Storm at Sea." There were displays of strange arts, such as glass blowing, and of new inventions, such as a knitting machine. Above all, there were the thousands and thousands of curios which Scudder's friends and agents, chiefly sea captains, had been harvesting for thirty years.

To these, Barnum added a series of "transient attractions": giants, jugglers, ventriloquists, "Il Studio, or Living Statues," albinos, educated dogs, rope-dancers, a rhinoceros and a giraffe, Indians in warpaint, "A Family of Industrious Fleas, taught by a Gentleman from Germany," fire-eaters, fat ladies, bearded ladies, and the first Punch and Judy show ever staged in America.

He also staged dog shows, flower shows, bird shows, poultry shows and baby shows. There was an "Aerial Garden"—two cedar plants, ten pots of wilted flowers and several small tables—where ice cream could be bought. In the Lecture Room, he produced "moral dramas" such as "The Drunkard," "Moses in Egypt," "The Hope of the Family," "Anna, or the Child of the Wreck" and "Joseph and his Brethren." (The Lecture Room was actually a theater, but was never referred to as such because of the New York theater's mucky reputation.) One of the most popular exhibits was THE GREAT MODEL OF NIAGARA FALLS WITH REAL WATER! The "great" model was only eighteen inches high, but honeymoon couples who could not afford a trip to the real falls were content to stare at the real water pouring over the small falls.

"Niagara" was merely one of Barnum's exaggerations, but soon he presented an exhibit which was utterly fraudulent. This was the "Fejee Mermaid"—a monkey's head and chest so cleverly sewn to a fish's body that the joint could not be detected. The composite was about three feet long. Its tail was twisted back, its arms were thrown up and its mouth was open, as if it had died in agony. It was black, ugly, and shriveled.

Moses Kimball, the proprietor of the Boston Museum, showed it to Barnum early in the summer of 1842. He said he had bought it from a sea captain who had paid $6,000 for it in Calcutta in 1817. Barnum's staff naturalist examined it. He saw that the monkey's hair was growing several inches down on the fish's "shoulders," and a microscope revealed what seemed to be tiny scales among the hair.

"I can't figure out how it was manufactured," he said. "It beats me."

Barnum asked, "Why assume it *is* manufactured?"

"Because I don't believe in mermaids."

"That's no reason at all," Barnum said. "*I'll* believe in it and I'll buy it."

Presently the *Herald* printed a report from Montgomery, Alabama, that Dr. J. Griffin, of the "London Lyceum of Natural History," had passed through town with "a most remarkable curiosity"—a veritable Fejee

Island mermaid, which he had purchased in China for the Lyceum's collection.

A week after the *Herald's* report, another New York newspaper carried a similar story, from Charleston, South Carolina. Dr. Griffin and his mermaid had appeared there, too. In due time, a third New York newspaper reported them in Washington. All three stories had been planted by Barnum, of course, and "Dr. Griffin" was as fictitious as the stories. It was now time to vitalize him. Accordingly, "Dr. Griffin, of Pernambuco for London," registered at a Philadelphia hotel, and was persuaded to give a glimpse of his mermaid to a number of reporters. Philadelphians with sharp eyes and long memories would have recognized the doctor as Levi Lyman, Barnum's old associate in the Joice Heth tour, but if any of them did so, they kept silent.

In New York, "Dr. Griffin" again allowed reporters to inspect the mermaid. The tide of curiosity was flooding, but Barnum was not yet ready to spread his net; he was still chumming the fishing grounds. He wrote a pamphlet about mermaids "proving" their authenticity, and put 10,000 copies on sale at a penny each—half their cost. Somewhere he procured three different engravings of mermaids, one of which he presented to each of three different newspapers along with a "scientific" description of the marvel. He explained to each editor that he had prepared the material to supplement Dr. Griffin's hoped-for appearance at the American Mu-

seum. Now, alas, that the Doctor had refused a public display, the material was of no use, unless by
chance . . . ? Each editor thought he had an "exclu-
sive," and when all three papers featured their mermaids on the same day, Barnum's glee burst out in one
of his puns: "They pronounced it a scaly trick!"

He kept the pun to himself; as yet, he was his own
and only audience. Although the tide was now full, he
still stayed hidden, lest his reputation for humbuggery
frighten the timid fish. Through an agent, he engaged
Concert Hall, on Broadway, and advertised that "In
accordance with numerous and urgent solicitations
from scientific gentlemen in this city," Dr. Griffin had
consented to exhibit his wondrous mermaid *"positively
for one week only!"* Now the fish—the suckers—fairly
jumped into Barnum's boat, at twenty-five cents
apiece. The week ended, but the rush continued so furiously that he ventured to reveal himself at last. He announced that the mermaid would thenceforth be on
exhibit at the American Museum "without extra
charge"—and let the public draw whatever conclusions
it liked.

As "Dr. Griffin" approached the Museum on the
morning of his début, he saw that Barnum had draped
its façade with a banner showing a mermaid eighteen
feet long. Lyman had not boggled at Joice Heth or at
representing himself as a director of the "London Lyceum of Natural History," but this banner was too

arrant an exaggeration for even him to countenance. He strode into Barnum's office and declared, "That flag must come in! Nobody can satisfy the public with our dried-up specimen, after exhibiting a picture representing it as eighteen feet! It's preposterous! I think I know something of the public 'swallow' by this time, and I tell you the mermaid won't go down if that flag remains up!"

Barnum protested, "It cost me over seventy dollars!"

Lyman buttoned his coat, walked to the door, and delivered his ultimatum: "Mr. Barnum, if *you* like to fight under that flag, you can, but I won't!"

Barnum could not spare "Dr. Griffin." He laughed and gave in, and the grave, courteous, distinguished "doctor" continued to deliver his "scientific" lecture.

In the four weeks immediately before the Mermaid's arrival, the Museum's receipts were $1,272. In the next four weeks, they were $3,341.93. Beyond any doubt, the Museum seemed headed for prosperity. The stimulus was not only the novelty of Barnum's exhibits, but the ingenuity, audacity and incessancy of his advertising. Night after night, until midnight or later, he would grind out items about the Museum, struggling to disguise blatant publicity pieces as legitimate news. Then would come the further struggle to persuade editors to print them. He wrote in his autobiography, "I thoroughly understood the art of advertising, not merely by means of printer's ink, which I have always used freely, and to which I confess myself so much indebted for my success, but by turning every possible circumstance to my account. I often seized upon an opportunity by instinct——"

One such opportunity came when a healthy-looking man begged Barnum for a job—any job at all—for a dollar a day. Inspiration kissed Barnum's forehead. He gave the man five ordinary bricks and told him, "Lay one on the sidewalk at the corner of Broadway and Anne. Lay another close by the Museum. Lay a third diagonally across the way, by the Astor House. Lay a fourth on the sidewalk in front of St. Paul's, opposite. Then take the fifth brick and march around the circuit, exchanging your brick at every point, and say nothing to anyone."

"Why?" the man asked.

"No matter," Barnum said. "All you need to know is that it brings you fifteen cents an hour. It's just a bit of my fun. You must seem deaf. Look serious. Answer no questions. Pay no attention to anyone. At the end of every hour by St. Paul's clock, show this ticket at the Museum door. Walk solemnly through every hall, leave, and do it over again."

The man began his round. Within half an hour, he had collected a convoy of 500 people. Within an hour, the sidewalk was packed. When St. Paul's clock struck, he entered the Museum, trailing a dozen people after him, toured all the exhibits, and resumed his

round. He did this for several days, until the police requested Barnum to call him in and relieve the conges-
tion.

"This trivial incident excited considerable talk and
amusement," Barnum boasted. "It advertised me and
it naturally advanced my purpose of making a lively
corner near the Museum."

To celebrate his first July 4th as manager, he
planned a string of American flags, as big and billowing
as mainsails, to run across Broadway from the roof of
the Museum to a tall tree in St. Paul's churchyard. But
when he asked permission of St. Paul's vestrymen, they
would have none of it. Barnum ordered his workmen to
string the flags anyhow, early on the morning of the
Fourth, and sure enough two vestrymen presently
stormed into his office, demanding satisfaction.

Barnum begged them to accompany him to the street.
There he pointed to the flags and pleaded, "Really,
gentlemen, they look very beautiful! They don't injure
your tree. I always stop my balcony music during your
services, and it's only fair for you to return the favor."
(His "balcony music" was a small band posted on a
balcony outside the Museum, where they raised such a
clangor that the public fled inside to escape.)

In vain. One of the vestrymen shouted, "If these
flags aren't taken down in ten minutes, I'll *cut* them
down!"

A crowd began to gather. Again Barnum "seized

upon an opportunity by instinct." Scowling, he rolled
up his sleeves and declared loudly, "Mister, I'd just like
to *see* you cut down the American flag on the Fourth of
July! You must be a Britisher!"

The crowd began to jostle the bewildered vestrymen. One of them murmured, "Oh, of course it's all
right," and they both filtered away.

Barnum never intended sacrilege. He was far too de-
vout, sincerely so. But where the interests of his beloved Museum were at stake, he tended to blind and
deafen himself to other considerations, even those of
the Church.

The circulating bricklayer and the huge American
flags were only a garnish on the steady, substantial fare
of banners, advertisements, posters, newspaper stories,
and show bills. All these were intended to lure customers into the Museum, but Barnum did not hesitate
to *drive* them in, as by his "Free Music for the Millions"
on the balcony.

Once inside, they created a new problem: how to get
them out. The Museum opened at sunrise and did not
close until late at night. Many country folk, arriving
early in New York, went from the station straight to
the Museum. Performances in the Lecture Hall were
continuous, and if a customer tired of moral drama, he
could wander at will among the other attractions and
stay as long as he liked. Families even brought picnic
baskets and spent the whole day, packing the rooms

and corridors and blocking off fresh cash. To meet this repeated emergency, Barnum nailed over a rear exit a large sign,

TO THE EGRESS

which lured his more ignorant customers out into the street before they knew what was happening.

So, by hook and somewhat by crook, Barnum hauled people in, stripped off their quarters, and eased them out. He and the Museum became such a popular topic that Olmsted dropped by the ticket office one July noon to see for himself how their investment was prospering.

Barnum was at his desk, munching a cold corned-beef sandwich he had brought from home that morning.

Olmsted asked, "Is this the way you eat dinner?"

Barnum said, "I haven't eaten a warm dinner since we bought the Museum, except on the Sabbath, and I never intend to eat another on a weekday until I'm out of debt."

Olmsted clapped him on the shoulder. "Then you're safe! You'll pay for the Museum before the year is out."

His prophecy was a few months premature. At the close of 1842, the Barnum family had succeeded in living on the $600 that Olmsted allowed them; and the

Museum's profits for the year had amounted to $27,916.32 as against $10,862 for 1841. But it was not until the next April that Barnum took title to the collection in his own name. At the same time, he also bought Peale's Museum, from the now bankrupt syndicate that had once engaged him as manager.

Much credit for the stride must go to his diligence, his ingenuity and his thrift. Much must also go to the happy chance which had recently led him to the greatest single act in the history of public entertainment.

General Tom Thumb

THE HAPPY CHANCE WAS A COLD SNAP THAT CAUGHT
Barnum in Albany in November, 1842. He had intended returning to New York by boat, but with the
Hudson frozen, he had to take a train. The Housatonic
Railroad's Albany-New York line ran through Bridgeport, so he stopped off for a night with his half-brother
Philo, who kept the Franklin Hotel. Their talk turned
to the Museum, of course, and Philo mentioned a local
curiosity, a young midget named Charlie Stratton. Taylor had heard of him; he might be worth seeing; could
Philo fetch him in? And presently Taylor was shaking
hands with the smallest child he had ever seen that
could walk alone.

Charlie would not be five years old until January 4th. He was less than two feet high and weighed

less than sixteen pounds. His foot was three inches long, and his hand was the size of a fifty-cent piece. His hair was pale blond, his eyes dark, his cheeks pink.

Looking at the manikin, Barnum must have reflected that whereas there had been no truth whatever in his claims for those utter humbugs, Joice Heth and the Fejee Mermaid, Charlie Stratton's *bona fides* was self-evident, for there he stood: alive, alert, healthy, cute, perfectly proportioned and incredibly minute.

Perfectly proportioned: Walter de la Mare might have had Charlie in mind when he wrote:

> Just a span and half a span
> From head to heel was this little man.
> Scarce a capful of small bones
> Raised up erect this Midget once.
> Yet not a knuckle was askew;
> Inches for feet God made him true.

Charlie was a midget—not a pygmy and not a dwarf. The distinction is important. Pygmies belong to special races of mankind, dark-skinned and primitive. Their average height is less than five feet, but they are not malformed. Their parents were pygmies and their children will be pygmies.

Dwarfs are common to all races. They are born dwarfs, with torsos normal or nearly so, but with short, thick, malformed limbs. Their parents were normal, and their children will be normal.

Midgets are also common to all races—commoner than is generally believed; there are perhaps 2,000 of them scattered around the world. They are not born midgets; they are normal at birth (Charlie had weighed 9 pounds, 2 ounces) and for several years afterward, until their pituitary gland stops functioning (Charlie's stopped when he was five months old). They are not malformed. Their parents were normal (Charlie's were), their brothers and sisters may be normal or midgets (Charlie's brother and two sisters were normal) and their children will be normal.

It is usual to think of freaks as foreign-born, but the Strattons were as thoroughly American as the Barnums. Charlie's mother liked to say, "He may be short of stature, but he's long on family. No one can ever look down on little Charles Sherwood Stratton!"

The first Stratton settled in Connecticut in 1682. Charlie's great-great-grandfather, Thomas, fought in the Revolution. Great-uncle Samuel was one of Bridgeport's leading citizens: a prosperous merchant, a banker, a judge of probate, senior warden in his church and Worshipful Master in his lodge. Charlie's father, Sherwood, was a carpenter; and his mother, Cynthia, helped in the kitchen of the Sterling House.

If the Sherwood Strattons had been as prosperous as the Samuel Strattons, they might not have consented to hiring Charlie out. But they did, for four weeks at three dollars a week (Barnum insisted on a short-term contract, lest the child suddenly sprout up), plus room and board for himself and his mother. Barnum arranged for them to live at his own house with Charity and his daughters (three of them now—Frances Irena had been born that spring), and there they arrived on Thanksgiving Day, December 8th.

It was an omen. In Charlie Stratton, who would make a fortune for him, Barnum had something for which he would be truly thankful all his life.

Cynthia Stratton's first response to New York was angry tears. Wherever she looked, she was affronted by banners and posters announcing "the rarest, the tiniest, the most diminutive dwarf imaginable—TOM THUMB, ELEVEN YEARS OLD AND ONLY TWENTY-FIVE INCHES HIGH, JUST ARRIVED FROM ENGLAND!!!"

Barnum explained to the outraged mother why this "Barnumizing" was necessary. As a name for a midget, "Charlie Stratton" radiated nothing, whereas "Tom Thumb" was irresistible, especially when coupled with the wildly incongruous title of "General." He was represented as "just arrived from England" in the hope that the deception might discourage America's "disgraceful preference for foreigners." And lastly, although Charlie was not quite five, he was being billed as eleven in order to suggest that he had stopped growing.

Mrs. Stratton reluctantly accepted Barnum's explanations, and Charlie's training began. He learned quickly. He had to; his début was only a week away. Barnum said, "He was an apt pupil with a great deal of native talent, and a keen sense of the ludicrous." His first lesson was in good manners: how to speak politely, shake hands, bow. Then he learned a few stage rôles, to point up the costumes Barnum had ordered. One was the uniform of a Continental soldier. In a white pigtail wig, a cocked hat, blue and red blouse, waistcoat, breeches, and boots the size of an iced-tea glass, Charlie drilled, saluted, and brandished his 10-inch sword. He had a clear, true voice, so he was also taught "Yankee Doodle" and another song or two.

Barnum's advertising did its work. A record crowd packed the Lecture Room on opening night. Barnum made a little speech of introduction, then Charlie trotted onstage and chirped his piece, with heavy emphasis on the puns that Barnum had written for him: "Good evening, ladies and gentlemen! I am only a Thumb, but a good hand in a general way at amusing you, for though a mite, I am mighty and can against all rivals bear off the palm. In short, don't make much of me, for making me more would be making me less. Though I grow in your favor, no taller I'd be. I'm great while I'm small, so I don't want to rise, but remain always General Tom Thumb in your eyes."

He strutted around, sang "Yankee Doodle," told a couple of jokes and trotted off. That was all, but the audience loved it. Five thousand people a week came to the Museum to see him. They followed him to the Lecture Room where he appeared at 3 P.M. and 7 P.M., and they followed him back to the Hall of Living Curiosities, where he appeared between times with an armless man, a fire-eater, a juggler, a fat boy and a snake charmer.

When his four weeks were up, Barnum gave him a new contract, for one year at seven dollars a week. And long before *that* was up, Barnum renewed again, at twenty-five dollars a week.

By now Charlie had expanded his act to include a repertory of poses after famous statues: Hercules and the Nemean Lion, Samson, Ajax Defying the Lightning, and so on. As Cupid, in gauzy wings and flesh-colored tights, he skipped about the stage, twanging his miniature bow and firing pencil-sized arrows across the footlights. Women battled for the arrows as souvenirs. They bought his photograph and showered him with presents and strained to cuddle him. When Barnum sent him on a tour that summer, 60,000 Southern women kissed him. But men liked him too. His pertness was attractive, not offensive. Philip Hone, the Mayor of New York, took his daughter to the Museum and wrote in his diary that Tom Thumb was "a handsome, well-proportioned little gentleman, lively, agreeable, sprightly, and talkative, with no deficiency of intellect. . . . The top of his head did not reach above my knee."

While Charlie was off touring, Barnum turned a quick trick at home. Privately, he bought a herd of fifteen yearling buffaloes for $700, and stabled them in a barn in New Jersey. With them he hired their former owner, C. D. French, who had driven them east, and presently—after seeding the press with false correspondence, Fejee Mermaid-style—it was announced via news stories, handbills and posters that a "Grand Buffalo Hunt, Free of Charge" would be held at the Hoboken Race Course on the afternoon of August 31st. Mr. French, "one of the most daring and experienced hunters of the West," would demonstrate his skill in hunting and with the lasso. Barnum's name was never mentioned.

Although the poor calves were anything but ferocious, the public was assured that it would be "protected" by a double railing around the whole course. As things turned out, the railing was not strong enough even so. The frightened calves broke through it and took shelter in a nearby swamp. However, French managed to lasso one and later exhibited some trick lassoing, and the good-humored crowd did not complain. After all, the anonymous benefactor had given them a free show with free music, and no one was out of pocket more than twelve and a half cents for his round-trip ferry fare from New York.

Free show? Then how did Barnum profit? Well, he had quietly chartered all the Hudson River ferryboats for the day, and each of 24,000 spectators paid him the round-trip fare. Second, he had leased out concessions for refreshment stands. Third, the publicity helped him stage a later "Grand Hunt" at Camden, across the river from Philadelphia. Fourth, he sold some of his herd in England and fattened the rest for buffalo steaks at 50 cents a pound. Fifth, he eventually let it leak out that the anonymous benefactor was that arch-humbug, the proprietor of the American Museum, and the "gratuitous advertising" that resulted was "enormous."

Meanwhile, Charlie was smashing attendance records wherever he went. City after city dubbed him "Darling!" "Delicious!" "Unique!" As the compliments and the cash poured in, Barnum dreamed of another, a vaster tour: a tour of Europe. If America adored Charlie so whole-heartedly, why wouldn't Europe adore him too? He broached his plan to Sherwood and Cynthia Stratton. "I'll give your son fifty dollars a week," he ended, "and I'll pay expenses for all three of you."

Fifty dollars a week! Twenty-six hundred a year! Carpentry had never brought in any such sum. The Strattons accepted.

Barnum booked passage for them on the packet *Yorkshire,* sailing on January 16, 1844. New Yorkers were so distressed at losing their pet that during his final weeks, they crowded into the Museum more thickly than ever—15,000 of them in a single day. His final morning, the *Sun* called him "the Wonderful Little Man" and cried affectionately, "Farewell, friend Thomas. . . . Mayest thou have prosperous gales and soon return!" The *Yorkshire* would sail at noon. Charlie stayed onstage until the last minute. The municipal brass band escorted him to the dock and played him aboard. The ship's bell rang, the band swung into "Home, Sweet Home," and Barnum began to weep.

6

At Queen Victoria's Court

BARNUM WEPT AGAIN IN LIVERPOOL, BUT FOR A DIFFER-
ent reason. The proprietor of a cheap waxworks called
on him and offered to engage Tom Thumb for ten dollars a week, admission to be three ha'pence. Barnum
said gloomily, "Dwarfs must be literally at a low figure
in England."

One evening he took Charlie to a Liverpool theater.
A couple in the next box struck up a conversation, and
when Barnum announced that he intended exhibiting
Charlie, and asked their advice about tickets, the lady
said enthusiastically, "The General is such a curiosity
I think you might put them as high as tuppence. Perhaps you—"

"No, no!" her husband interrupted. "You'd never

succeed! Make it a penny. That's the usual price for seeing giants and midgets here."

Barnum winced but declared, "Never shall the price be less than a shilling sterling, and some of the nobility and gentry will pay *gold!*"

He was whistling past the graveyard of his hopes. His brash and naive plan had been to head straight for London and make his headquarters at Buckingham Palace. Alas, Prince Albert's father, the Duke of Saxe-Coburg, had just died and the court had gone into mourning. Atop these dreary circumstances, Barnum was a stranger in a foreign land. He was homesick and heartsick for a familiar face. And he was cold.

There in his gloomy hotel, Barnum cried for the second time. It was probably the last fit of utter despair in his life and it did not last long. In a few days, he took his little troupe to London and booked the General for three nights at the Royal Princess's Theatre. Success was instantaneous and overwhelming. But although the theater offered a re-engagement at a much higher salary, Barnum turned it down. He wanted to bring the General before the public himself, and in his own time and way.

His way was to rent Lord Talbot's mansion in fashionable Grafton Street, and have the General send the press, the peerage, and Parliament formal invitations to call. Those who accepted spread the tidings among their friends. But when the friends ventured to call, too, Barnum's butler turned them away.

"I had not yet announced a public exhibition," Barnum said, "and as a private American gentleman, it became me to maintain the dignity of my position." For all his feigned haughtiness, however, he was careful to see that his butler took the name of everyone refused admission and that an invitation was sent him promptly.

Barnum's false snobbishness was the perfect tactic. Word of the General swept London. Within a week, Baroness Rothschild, the wife of the great international banker, was begging Barnum to bring him to her house. They stayed two hours and as they retired, a fat purse was slipped into Barnum's hand. The dark days were ended. Said Barnum, "The golden shower has begun to fall."

It had indeed. He engaged Egyptian Hall in Piccadilly and threw the doors open to all comers at a shilling a head. Again the General was a stupendous success; and for the first time since they had left home, Sherwood Stratton, taking tickets, stopped longing for the friendly streets of Bridgeport. Barnum had only one disappointment: he had not yet harnessed Queen Victoria to his triumphal chariot of publicity.

That came now. Through a letter of introduction from the editor of *The New York Tribune,* Horace Greeley, Barnum met the American Minister to Great Britain, Edward Everett, and through him he met Charles Murray, the Master of the Queen's Household.

Murray had written a book, and Barnum happened

to have read it. He massaged the proud author with compliments, then mentioned slyly that he and the General were about to begin a tour of the Continent— although they would be glad to postpone it, of course, if there were a chance of meeting the Queen.

Next morning, a towering Life Guard in full scarlet uniform brought Barnum an invitation to present himself and General Tom Thumb at Buckingham Palace on the evening of March twenty-third. When the great day came, Barnum posted a sign on the door of Egyptian Hall:

> **Closed this evening,**
> **General Tom Thumb**
> **Being at Buckingham Palace**
> **By command of**
> **Her Majesty**

The storekeeper's son from Bethel and the carpenter's son from Bridgeport—two Connecticut Yankees—were off to Queen Victoria's Court.

Barnum wore knee breeches, with white silk stockings and buckled pumps. Charlie was also in court dress, of brown velvet with cut steel buttons, a white frilled shirt, a cocked hat, and a sword about the size of a paper knife. Awaiting them at the far end of the picture gallery were the Queen, her Consort, her beautiful mother and twenty or thirty others. Charlie bowed and said, "Good evening, ladies and gentlemen!"

The court laughed. The young Queen (she was not quite twenty-five) was in mourning, with no jewelry except her wedding ring. She took Charlie's hand and showed him around the gallery.

"Your pictures are first-rate," he told her. "But where's your little boy?"

She said the Prince of Wales* had gone to bed; the General would see him at another time.

Then Charlie went into his act. He impersonated Napoleon, ran through his repertory of Grecian statues, danced a hornpipe, and sang several songs, including one larded with the puns that Barnum so enjoyed. Its last stanza was,

> *You'd think, from his exertions*
> *That his weary limbs and head*
> *Much rest required, yet Tom never*
> *Could lay long in his bed.*
> *To realize a fortune*
> *In a little time he ought,*
> *He's coining money daily,*
> *Although he's dreadful short.*

It had been explained to Barnum that when he and the General withdrew, etiquette required them to back out. A gentleman-in-waiting now caught his eye, and the withdrawal began. Barnum managed excellently, but the gallery was 150 feet long, and little Charlie had

* Later King Edward VII.

to back a few steps, then turn and run to catch up, then turn and bow, and back a few steps more. The Queen's poodle became so excited that it began snapping at Charlie's heels, and he had to defend himself with his bodkin-sword. At last they made it safely to an ante-room, where an attendant brought them a purse, with Her Majesty's hope that the General had not been injured. The gentleman-in-waiting expressed the same hope, lest, he added archly, "any affront to so renowned a personage provoke the United States to a declaration of war." Supper was served them, and the climax of their evening came when the editor of the *Court Circular* allowed Barnum to dictate an account of their audience for publication next day.

Barnum had read the English aright: where royalty and the nobility lead, the crowd is quick to follow. "This notice of my visit to the Queen," he wrote proudly, "wonderfully increased the attraction of my exhibition, and compelled me to obtain a more commodious hall." Admissions shot up to an average of 2,000 a day, or $500. Moreover, several times a week, after the General's regular evening performance, Barnum would book him into private houses at $50 an appearance. *Punch* dubbed him "The Pet of the Palace." Songs were written about him, dances were named after him, children played with Tom Thumb paper dolls.

Two weeks after their first audience, the Queen sent

for them again. This time she received them in the presence of the Queen of the Belgians, the Princess Royal,* aged three and a half, and the Prince of Wales, a year younger. Charlie remarked to the Queen, "I've seen you before, Ma'am," and matched heights with the Prince, observing cockily, "He's taller than I am, but I *feel* as big as anybody."

After his performance, the Queen gave him a medallion of gold and mother-of-pearl, set with precious stones. On one side were the crown and the royal initials, V.R., and on the reverse, a bouquet of flowers in rubies. Later she sent him boxes of candy, a feather for his Highland bonnet and a mother-of-pearl case for his visiting cards, which were the size of postage stamps.

The inventory of his presents soon began to sound like a fashionable jeweler's. Dowager Queen Adelaide gave him a gold watch with a long gold chain; the Duke of Devonshire gave him a gold snuff box set with turquoises; and there were jeweled swords, pistols and canes almost past counting. Barnum put them all on display at Egyptian Hall, identifying each with its illustrious donor.

On Charlie's third visit to the Palace, when Queen Victoria invited him to meet her Uncle Leopold, the King of the Belgians, he made bold to hint at a present more to his personal taste. The song he chose

* Later the mother of Kaiser Wilhelm II.

was "Yankee Doodle," despite Barnum's frown, and at the lines

Yankee Doodle went to town,
Riding on a pony,

he pointed out the window to a pony he had spied in the courtyard, then pointed back to himself. The Queen either missed the hint or refused to act on it. What she gave him was a gold pencil case—because, she explained, "You once told me you liked to draw." She hadn't caught the point. What the General had said was, "I like to draw and I do it very well." It was one of his and Barnum's puns. He meant, "to draw crowds to the show."

He was a saucy little rascal. When Queen Adelaide remarked, "You look very smart today, General," he replied smugly, "I guess I do." And when the great Duke of Wellington asked what he was thinking about during his impersonation of Napoleon, the General told him, "The loss of Waterloo." The saucier he became, the better his exalted patrons seemed to like it, perhaps because no one else ever dared be flip with them. His special performances were not exclusively for celebrities. Barnum took care to see that he made many visits, without charge, to orphanages and hospitals.

In October, 1844, Barnum made a quick trip home. He wanted to extend his lease on the Museum building for five years more, even though his original lease with Mr. Olmsted still had three years to run. He also wanted to bring back with him Charity and his two older daughters, Caroline and Helen. The youngest, Frances Irena, had died in April just before her second birthday.

On January 1, to celebrate both the New Year and, three days later, Charlie's birthday, Barnum gave him as a present an equal partnership. The seven-year-old boy would henceforth net better than $100,000 a year.

7

A Triumphal Tour of the Continent

IN FEBRUARY, 1845, BARNUM CROSSED TO PARIS TO BUY
some new marvels for the Museum and to lay a red
carpet for the General's early arrival.

From Houdin, the great magician, he bought a mechanical artist, "an ingenious little figure which sat at a
table and if asked for an emblem of fidelity, instantly
drew a handsome dog." He reserved hotel rooms for
the company, engaged a tutor for Charlie and an interpreter for himself, and leased an exhibition hall.
He paid his respects to the American Minister. To test
the tone of the Paris press, and the response of the city,
he struck a few tentative chords of publicity. Best of
all, he made a happy arrangement with the government bureau which licensed all entertainments.

The Paris hospitals were beneficiaries, by law, of a tax of 11 per cent on the gross receipts of a theater, but of 25 per cent on those of a freak or natural curiosity. Barnum, tortured by the prospect of surrendering a quarter of his receipts, persuaded the bureau to give him a contract for two months, in return for a flat 2,000 francs paid in advance. Both parties were pleased with the deal. The bureau "knew" that no mere midget could possibly attract 4,000 francs in admissions in a month, and Barnum knew that Charlie would attract almost that much in a single day. Events would prove Barnum's estimate much more nearly accurate, to the anguish of the bureau, which complained of his "Yankee trick."

He went back to London, collected his troupe and brought it to Paris. Here there was no waiting for royalty's invitation. It arrived the very next day, requesting Monsieur Barnum and General Tom Thumb to present themselves at the Tuileries Palace the following Sunday. The Queen of the Belgians was King Louis Philippe's daughter; she had seen the General at Buckingham Palace, and quite probably she had recommended him to her father. In any event, the King was there with almost his entire family.

Also present was the editor of the official *Journal des Débats* who reported the audience enthusiastically in the next day's paper. He described the General's performance and his costumes—all but one: "We will not mention a celebrated uniform which he wore in

London, and which was amazingly successful with our oversea neighbors. Tom Thumb had too much taste to take this costume to the Tuileries. We hope that while he sojourns in Paris he will leave it at the bottom of his portmanteau."

The King kept Barnum and Charlie for two hours. He gave Charlie an emerald brooch set with diamonds, told him he had slept in Indian wigwams during his exile in America, and was so warm and friendly that Barnum was emboldened to ask a favor: On Longchamps Day, the big social fête, might the General's small carriage-and-four join the procession along the Champs Elysées with the equipages of the court and diplomatic corps? Otherwise, it might be crushed by the crowd. The King consented.

Barnum had had one carriage built for Charlie in Bridgeport in 1843, but he had commissioned a new one in London from a carriage-builder "by appointment to the Queen." It was a four-wheeler, with a body eleven inches wide and twenty high, painted red, white and blue. The door handles, hub caps and lamp brackets were silver. The plate-glass windows had Venetian blinds. The cushions were covered with yellow silk. The panels of the doors displayed Britannia and the Goddess of Liberty, supported by the British lion and the American eagle, with the motto, "Go Ahead!"

It had cost $1,500, not counting the four matched Shetland ponies (each thirty-four inches high in its silver-mounted harness) or the tailored liveries of the eight-year-old coachman and seven-year-old footman: cocked hats and wigs, sky-blue coats trimmed with silver lace, red breeches, white stockings, and silver buckles and garters.

When this "elegant turnout" appeared on Longchamps Day, with the General bowing right and left, Barnum acknowledged that there was never such an advertisement. The crowds cheered "Général Tom Pouce" again and again. And when, shortly afterwards, Barnum opened his exhibition, he took in $1,100 the first day. He would have doubled his profits if the hall had been larger.

A fashionable café changed its name to "Tom Pouce" and mounted a life-size figure of the General over its door. The leading ladies of the Court, society and the stage came to kiss him. Songs were written about him. Artists begged him to sit for them. There was a sudden fad for snuff-boxes with his picture on the lid. Every shop window showed his statuette in plaster, clay or chocolate. He was elected to the French Dramatic Society, on the strength of his performance in "Le Petit Poucet" ("The Little Thumb"), a five-act comedy written for him especially. So enormous was his popularity that tickets were reserved two months in advance, and Barnum had to hire a cab every night to carry home the receipts.

The Court sent for them three times. The King particularly enjoyed a song in which the General acknowledged his and America's debt to France for her help

during the struggle for independence, but feared that
the charming Parisiennes would cost him his own. On
his last visit to the Court, the King ordered him to
unpack the costume "at the bottom of his portmanteau" and give his impersonation of Napoleon. He did
so to great applause, but in great secrecy. Barnum did
not want to risk offending France's pride, so no word
reached the newspapers.

After three booming months in Paris, the troupe
started on a circuit of southern France. They traveled in
two carriages, with a third to carry their baggage and
the General's own carriage-and-four. All this elaborate,
expensive organization to exhibit a person weighing
but fifteen pounds? Said Barnum: "When the General's retinue passed along the roads, and especially
when it came into a town, people naturally and eagerly
inquired what great personage was on his travels. And
when told that it was 'the celebrated General Tom
Thumb and suite,' everybody desired to go and see
him. It was thus the best advertising we could have
had."

Barnum was trying a new technique now. After engaging a hall and posting an announcement of their arrival, he directed all his energies *apparently* toward
keeping the townsfolk quiet. He begged them not to get
excited. He assured them that they would have every
opportunity to see the little General and that if one
exhibition did not suffice, two or even three would be
given.

"Strange as it may seem," Barnum wrote, "people who were told to keep quiet would get terribly excited, and when the General arrived excitement would be at fever heat . . . and the treasury filled!"

They must have been happy, bowling through the beautiful French countryside in the lushness of full summer. They were making money almost as fast as they could count it. Barnum practiced his French until he was quite fluent, though less so than Charlie. And somewhere along the road occurred a scene which some artist should have caught and fixed forever: Barnum stripped off his shoes and socks, and trod out half a barrel of grapes, to the sound of a fiddle!

They dipped into Spain and performed for the Royal Family at Pamplona, where fifteen-year-old Queen Isabella gave Charlie a miniature of herself on a gold chain, set with diamonds and sapphires. Then they headed north for Belgium. When they crossed the frontier at Courtrai, their "superb establishment," as Barnum referred to it, led the Belgian customs officials to enquire what rank the distinguished traveler held in his own country.

Someone replied, "He is Prince Charles Stratton of the Dukedom of Bridgeport, in the Kingdom of Connecticut."

The officials reverently raised their hats.

The day after their arrival in Brussels, they were summoned to Laeken Palace to perform for King Leopold, Queen Louise, and the royal children. Waterloo was only sixteen miles from Brussels, so Barnum made up a party and drove out to the battlefield. It was exactly the sort of expedition he enjoyed. He asked the guide to show him where "Captain Tippitiwichet, of the Connecticut Fusiliers" and other imaginary friends had met their deaths. Another guide sold him for his museum a strap of leather from the boot that Lord Uxbridge, commander of the British cavalry, was wearing when a cannon ball took his leg off. Barnum was quite sure that the concessionaire had purchased all the cast-off boots in Brussels and its vicinity, but he didn't mind. He also bought pistols, bullets and buttons. Several months later, on a visit to Birmingham, England, he was taken through a factory which shipped barrels of "relics" to Waterloo every year. Barnum said sadly, "Our purchases looked rather cheap!"

They returned to London in the spring of 1846. Barnum booked the General into Egyptian Hall again, and also into Douglass' Standard Theatre, where he starred in "Hop-o'-my-Thumb; or the Seven League Boots," an English adaptation of "Le Petit Poucet."

The General played three months in London. As summer approached, Barnum took him on a tour of England, Scotland and Ireland. They enjoyed the English countryside as much as they had France. The Oxford students gravely insisted on paying their admissions in farthings, forty-eight to a shilling—the smallest coin, they argued, to see the smallest man.

At Warwick, Barnum spied an advertisement for two "Canadian Giantesses, each seven feet in height," and planned to engage them for the Museum if they weren't humbugs. He twitched up one's skirt, and she knocked him spinning, but not before he saw that she was standing on an eighteen-inch pedestal.

Charlie polished his Highland accent for Scotland, and sang a topical song to great applause:

Goliath was a tall man, and William Wallace too,
I'm not so tall as either, nor yet as high as you,
I just came out before you to sing a little song,
I hope my short acquaintance will be remembered long.

In Dublin, Sherwood Stratton took in $1,501 on the last night.

They returned to London for another engagement at Egyptian Hall, with Charlie doubling at the Surrey Zoological Gardens. There, a stunt of Barnum's nearly went tragically awry. He put Charlie in a captive balloon, so that the audience would have a better look at him. But one windy October afternoon a sudden gust just missed tearing it away, and Charlie was grounded from then on.

Iranistan,
Show Place of Bridgeport

THE TROUPE SAILED HOME FROM ENGLAND IN FEBRUARY 1847, almost exactly three years after their first arrival. Barnum gave Charlie a few days' rest in New York before presenting him at the Museum with a fanfare of capitals and italics:

"Patronized by all the CROWNED HEADS of Europe . . . seen by over 5,000,000 persons . . . GRAND DEBUT . . . *extensive preparations* . . . COURT DRESS from Queen Victoria, of England . . . BEAUTIFUL SCOTCH COSTUME . . . *magnificent presents!*"

Charlie drew such crowds as had never been seen before. Mayor Hone of New York City recorded in his diary, "He is making here a thousand dollars a day. He performs four or five times each day to a thousand or twelve hundred persons. He kisses the goodlooking women and in one way or another sends his audience away well satisfied."

Four weeks of it was enough. Charlie had been working for four and a half years and had earned a holiday. Barnum took him home and let him give two benefit performances for the Bridgeport Ladies' Charitable Society, then turned him loose for a month of doing nothing, in the relaxing company of his old dog Alex.

Barnum wrote, summing up their tour, "The General left America a diffident, uncultivated little boy [of six]; he came back an educated little man [of nine]."

He had learned to speak French and Spanish, and to strum the piano and saw the violin. He had begun to smoke cigars and sip weak wine. He was a gay, witty conversationalist. He was rich; a London newspaper quoted his "secretary" as setting his European receipts at $750,000. In fact, he had not changed in only one respect: his size. He still was only twenty-five inches tall and he still weighed only fifteen pounds.

While Charlie rested, Barnum was busy arranging displays of the curiosities he had bought abroad. One of the most popular was Houdin's mechanical artist. England contributed "The Happy Family," a congregation of some 200 birds and animals all in one cage. Another English act was a company of seven bell ringers. Although the men came from Lancashire, Barnum insisted that they grow moustaches, wear a picturesque costume, and bill themselves as "Swiss." He had bid for three other English attractions, but had not been able to get them. One was Madame Tussaud's famous waxworks. Another was Shakespeare's house, from Stratford-on-Avon. English pride was aroused in the nick of time. "Had they slept a few days longer," Barnum claimed, he would have had it. The third was a tree on which Lord Byron had carved his name. Barnum offered £500 for it, but the outraged owner refused to sell.

Barnum could have offered ten or even fifty times as much—and paid it—without anxiety. If Charlie Stratton was rich, he had made his manager richer. Barnum used to pat Charlie's head and say, "That's my piece of goods! I've sold it hundreds of thousands of times and never delivered it yet!" A steady cataract of money was deluging his New York Museum. Its receipts for one day now were higher than they had been weekly, and he had branched out with another museum, in Baltimore. He was famous, too—chiefly, of course, as a showman, but also as a newspaper correspondent. During his three years in Europe, he had written roughly 100 news-letters for the New York *Atlas*.

He liked to tell how, about this time, he was sitting in his office one day when a man bought a ticket and asked the box-office clerk if Mr. Barnum was in the Museum. The clerk pointed to him: "This is Mr. Barnum."

The visitor inspected him thoroughly and at leisure. "Never mind the Museum," he said. "I've had my money's worth," and walked out.

Not that Barnum's appearance was odd in any way. He was a big man with a big head and big features. At thirty-six, his curly hair was thinning along the part. Two heavy grooves ran from his nose to the corners of his mouth. Most of his pictures show his lips shut tight. His clothes were rich but quiet; his ruffled shirts and satin cravats were the style of the day. He wore a plain gold ring on his left hand, and a long, thin gold chain across his waistcoat. He looked like a man of dignity and substance, and so he was.

When Charlie's vacation was up, Barnum took him on another tour. It began in Washington, with a formal call on President and Mrs. Polk, then went to Richmond, then up the East Coast for a swing around New England and over to Portland, Maine. Daily expenses averaged less than $30; daily receipts averaged about $500.

Charlie had another vacation in the early fall before he and Barnum were off again, through the Southern cities, to Havana in January, back to New Orleans, and up the Mississippi. They reached Pittsburgh early in May and there they parted—Charlie to continue the tour with his parents and with Barnum's representatives, and Barnum himself to return to Connecticut.

"I had now been a straggler from home for 13 years," he wrote, "and I cannot describe the feeling of gratitude with which I reflected that I would henceforth spend my days in the bosom of my family. [There was a new daughter now, Pauline Taylor, born on March 1, 1846.] I reached my residence in Bridgeport in the latter part of May——"

This residence, Iranistan (pronounced *I'*-ran-*IS"*-tan), had been building for two years and was finished at last. Barnum had picked Bridgeport as the site because it was convenient to New York, it was on the water, and its bustle promised to make it the most important city in Connecticut. He had picked the design —a bizarre miscellany of domes, spires, piazzas and lattices adapted from George IV's Pavilion at Brighton— because "a pile of buildings of a novel order might indirectly serve as an advertisement of my Museum." (It stood in full view of the railroad tracks.) And he had picked the name "Iranistan" because it means "Oriental villa." A New York editor preferred his own explanation: *"I-ran-a-long-time-before I could stan'."*

Reindeer and elk roamed through the seventeen-acre park. Fountains played under the transplanted trees. The stables, conservatories and out-buildings were applauded as "perfect in their kind."

The main house was 124 feet along the front and three stories high—ninety feet to the top of the central dome, which enclosed an observatory sixty feet in circumference. The downstairs was a gleam of rosewood and a glare of Florentine marble. Barnum boasted that appropriate furniture was made expressly for every room; some of it was carved with snakes, birds and dolphins. Hardly a critic failed to note that his study, hung with orange satin, opened on to a shower with *"hot and cold water!"*

To build and furnish Iranistan cost the enormous sum of $200,000. Here, on November 14, 1848, the Barnums had a housewarming for nearly a thousand guests. One of them gazed his fill, then paid the highest compliment at his command: "It's as elegant as a steamboat!"

Barnum often said that this year and the next were the happiest in his life. He commuted to New York every week to deal with the affairs of the Museum, but the attention it had once monopolized it now shared with his family and with local activities in Bridgeport. The Fairfield County Agricultural Society elected him president. He was no farmer, but he had several pieces of acreage in the neighborhood, and he raised fruit and vegetables on one, and chickens on another. A third, he fenced in and stocked with the overflow of elk and reindeer from Iranistan. This lot adjoined the property of one of his friends, who posted a notice:

ALL PERSONS ARE FORBID TRESPASSING ON THESE GROUNDS, OR DISTURBING THE DEER.

J. D. JOHNSON

Johnson was greatly pleased with his "score" until a few days later, when he saw that Barnum had added, under his name, "Game-keeper to P. T. Barnum."

Two incidents from General Tom Thumb's recent tour now loomed large in Barnum's life. One had happened in the fall of 1847, when they were playing Saratoga Springs, New York. There Barnum saw "so much intoxication among men of wealth and intellect, filling the highest positions in society, that I began to ask myself, What guarantee is there that *I* may not become a drunkard? Although I was not in the habit of partaking often of strong drink, I pledged myself at that time never again to partake of any kind of spirituous liquors." He excepted wines and beers from this first pledge, but the following year he knocked off the neck of every bottle in the Iranistan cellars, and swore himself to absolute teetotalism. (Later he gave up tobacco, too.)

From that moment, temperance had no more vigorous advocate than P. T. Barnum. He preached it, wrote it, lived it. When he brought Jenny Lind to America in 1850, and she toasted him in a glass of wine at their first dinner together, he astonished her by saying, "Miss Lind, I don't think you can ask any other favor on earth which I wouldn't gladly grant, but I'm a teetotaler and I must beg to be permitted to drink your health and happiness in a glass of cold water."

He used his Museum to promote temperance by banning the sale of liquor, by presenting "The Moral,

Domestic Drama of The Drunkard, or The Fallen Saved," and by inviting members of the audience to come to the box office and sign a teetotal pledge. So deep was his conviction that, having estimated the yearly retail sale of liquor in New York City at $25,-500,000, he publicly offered—in return for that sum and the suspension of liquor sales for one year—to pay all the city taxes; send every child to a good school; give every woman a silk dress and every man a broadcloth suit; every family three barrels of flour and 100 good books; and every person, male or female, young or old, a ticket to his Museum. (For all his fervor, Barnum never forgot to plug the Museum.) His offer was sincere—and good publicity—but the city declined it.

The second incident had happened in the spring of 1848, at Cincinnati. A poster advertising a freak horse caught Barnum's eye, so he dropped in to see it. The horse was normal in color, conformation and size, though smallish, but its coat was thick and curly, like a sheep's, whereas its tail was almost hairless, and it had no mane at all.

Barnum smelled money. He bought the horse and sent it to Bridgeport until he could find the right bait. He found it that winter, when Col. John Charles Frémont's expedition to California was temporarily lost in the San Juan mountains of Colorado. Frémont was a national hero, and the whole nation was anxious about him. Moreover, any event on the frontier was doubly interesting in those days. Barnum realized this—hence the popularity of his "Grand Buffalo Hunt" and, soon afterwards, of New York's first Wild West show, which a band of Iowa Indians staged in the Moral Lecture Room. So out of its barn at Bridgeport now came the Woolly Horse, gaitered and cloaked to hide its wool, and down to a private stable in New York it went, while the moment ripened.

In a few weeks, Frémont was reported safe, and Barnum immediately began grinding out "despatches" to the New York newspapers—the same technique he had used with the Fejee Mermaid. The despatches reported that near the Gila River, Frémont had captured an extraordinary animal which he was forwarding to the Quartermaster General: curly coat, no hair on its tail, no mane. Presently the same papers announced that "COL. FRÉMONT'S NONDESCRIPT OR WOOLLY HORSE" would be on exhibit for a few days "previous to his departure for London. Nature seems to have exerted all her ingenuity in the production of this astounding animal. . . . It has the haunches of a Deer, the tail of the Elephant, a fine curled wool of camel's hair color, and easily bounds twelve or fifteen feet high."

The showroom was at Broadway and Reade Street, not at the Museum. The advertisements never mentioned the Museum nor Barnum; he was hiding his hand, as when he presented the Buffalo Hunt and the Mermaid. The Woolly Horse eventually made its way to Washington. Here it caused a controversy which Barnum turned to his advantage, as usual. Colonel Frémont's father-in-law, Senator Thomas Hart Benton of Missouri, flatly declared that Frémont had never seen the horse; Barnum's agent was therefore guilty of fraud, and the Senator was suing for the return of his twenty-five cents admission. The case was dismissed, but not before Barnum had transmuted the publicity into dollars. When the silver stream at last dried up, he admitted the hoax and put the Woolly Horse out to pasture at Iranistan as an advertisement for the Museum.

Only a few months before, Barnum had denounced "the whirlpool of business excitement" and had pined for a chance to rest. Doubtless he sighed so pitifully and rolled his eyes so pathetically that anyone who did not know him might have believed he meant it. But though he had forsworn intoxicating liquors, his intoxicating profession he could never forswear. Indeed, even as he pined, he was planning a "Congress of Nations," which would comprise "a man and woman, as perfect as could be procured, from every accessible people, civilized and barbarous, on the face of the globe." In addition, he was selling a branch museum in Baltimore, buying one in Philadelphia, and preparing an illustrated guide to the one in New York.

But far more important than all these other deals combined, he was also promoting an enterprise so daring that in retrospect he trembled at his own audacity. It was an attraction that would raise America's fever as high as had Tom Thumb, would double Barnum's fortune, and would rivet his title as "The World's Greatest Showman." His attraction was Jenny Lind.

Jenny Lind

IT WOULD BE DIFFICULT TO FIND ANYONE MORE APTLY
named than Jenny Lind. She had been christened Jo-
hanna Maria, but once the warm little "Jenny" was
attached to her, perfectly reflecting her demure simplicity, it stayed forever. It is the name on her tomb-
stone. She was born in Stockholm on October 6, 1820,
the daughter of an improvident bookkeeper (some say
a lace-maker) and a schoolmistress. At the age of three,
she could pick out a tune on the piano. At nine, a
ballerina's maid overheard her singing, and presently
she was under contract to the Royal Theatre.

She was never a beauty or even close to it. Her features were expressive, her movements graceful, her
figure slender, but there was an unappetizing pallor
over all: pale eyes, pale hair, pale complexion. Her

own description of her young self was "small, ugly, broad-nosed, shy, gauche, under-grown." ("The Ugly Duckling," by her friend Hans Christian Andersen, was her favorite of all his stories.) Yet with looks so insipid, and despite her clear, true voice, it was as an actress, not as a singer, that she began her career at the age of ten.

Jenny did not sing professionally until she was seventeen. The date, March 7, she observed for the rest of her life as a second birthday, the birthday of her art. Europe's most famous *maestro*, Manuel Garcia of Paris, put the finishing touches on her voice. Before her ten months' training with him, her reputation did not extend beyond Sweden. Now it burst the frontiers, and "The Bird of the Northland," "The Queen of Song," "The Swedish Nightingale," was suddenly famous throughout Denmark, Germany, Austria, and England. (She considered France wicked and sang there only once, at a charity concert in Nice, late in her life.)

Her voice was a soprano that reached from low D to high F. Chopin said, "Her singing is pure and true; the charm of her soft passages is beyond description." Mendelssohn accompanied her on the piano when she sang in Leipzig in 1845, and wrote his "Elijah" for her —"as great an artist as ever lived; and the greatest I have known." Wagner, Berlioz and Schubert were hardly less laudatory.

There were, to be sure, a few dissenting opinions, most of them by writers. Thackeray was "thinking of something else the whole time she was jugulating away." Hawthorne was "not very much interested in her." Walt Whitman grunted, "There was a vacuum in the head of the performance. Beauty pervaded it no doubt, and that of a high order. It was the beauty of Adam before God breathed into his nostrils." Carlyle objected that her program was "mere nonsense." He said, "I do not design to hear Lind again; it would not bring me sixpence worth of benefit, I think, to hear her sing six months in that kind of material."

Carlyle's charge and Whitman's were the two most often leveled against her: a second-rate program, rendered without depth and passion. All adverse criticism, however, was smashed and swept away in the tidal wave of adulation that inundated Europe. The like would not be seen again until Lindbergh landed there in 1927.

When the theatre doors were opened for her London début, in Meyerbeer's "Robert le Diable" in May 1847, the stampede for seats was so furious that clothes were torn and people were injured. It was called "the Jenny Lind crush," another symptom of "the Jenny Lind fever." A song about it began:

Of manias we've had many, and some have raised the wind,
But the tallest far of any, is that for Jenny Lind . . .
*My wife has a Jenny Lind bonnet, and a Jenny Lind visite;**
With Jenny's portrait on it, my handkerchief looks neat.
Yes, all is Jenny Lind, now—in every shop she's found;

* A cap made of silk or lace.

Jenny Lind you get there retail, by the yard, quart, pint or
    pound . . .
O Jenny, when you leave us, what shall we ever do,
To catch another Nightingale to sing as sweet as you?

The nightingale's nest, said *Punch*, was "in the wide world's heart." Further, *Punch* recommended that, in view of a current gold shortage, tickets to her concerts be accepted as legal tender and called "Jenny Lind scrip."

Jenny made a tour of England that autumn, and at Norwich she met Bishop Edward Stanley, who had a massive influence on her career. Her strict, puritanical upbringing, which would not permit her even to travel on Sundays, had made her view the operatic stage with the primmest misgivings. Indeed, she consented to continue in operatic rôles only because they offered the shortest route to her heart's desire: endowment of a Stockholm hospital for poor children. Her determination to renounce opera was strengthened by her companions and friends, including Bishop Stanley. The good bishop seems to have been better qualified to appreciate the purity of her soul than that of her voice, for after hearing her sing "Angels Ever Bright and Fair" in his drawing room, he told her, "Such beautiful words! If you would only say them without the notes!"

She once declared that she had met only two completely honest men in her life. Bishop Stanley was one. The other was her son, who interrupted her practice

one day by saying, "Mother, *do* stop that scream-
ing!"

In the spring of 1849, after frenzied triumphs in
Berlin and Stockholm, she announced that May 10
would mark her final appearance in an operatic rôle:
Alice, in "Robert le Diable" at Her Majesty's Theatre,
London. Her generosity to local charities had pre-
vented her from reaching the total endowment she had
set for her hospital, but her distaste for the stage had
now hardened to the point where she could no longer
expose herself to its "vice and intrigue." She sang her
last Alice and retired to Lübeck, Germany, for rest
and for a diet based on milk and grapes. There Barnum's agent found her in December and offered her a
contract to come to America.

Barnum and Tom Thumb had left London a few
months before Jenny's first arrival, so he had never
heard what *Punch* called "the marvelous voice, un-
eclipsed in its glory." It would have made little differ-
ence. His only known comment on her singing suggests
that, like Bishop Stanley, his forte was not music. She
had just finished "Lo, Hear the Gentle Lark!", and
Barnum whispered to a neighbor, "O.K., I guess, but
she can't imitate a flute like those little didappers I
used to hear on Putnam Lake when I was a young
'un!" One of his boyhood friends wrote of a Danbury
"social" in 1831, "Taylor was the worst singer of us all
when we attempted 'All Hail the Power of Jesus'
Name'." Although he couldn't even carry a tune, he

used to go to church with Horace Greeley, on Sundays when they were both in New York, and Barnum would screech the hymns in a loud, flat voice that made the neighbors wince.

No, enchantment by Jenny's virtuosity had nothing to do with his offer. It was inspired by two entirely different considerations. These were, in his own words, "1st. The chances were greatly in favor of immense pecuniary success; and 2d. Inasmuch as the American public suspect that my capacities do not extend beyond the power to exhibit a stuffed monkey-skin or a dead mermaid, I can afford to lose fifty thousand dollars in bringing to this country the greatest musical wonder in the world."

It is difficult to say which consideration was the more important. Barnum always melted in the warm presence of a dollar; but by now, thanks to Tom Thumb, he had piled up enough of them to assure a wolf-free door, and he could afford to turn his thoughts from such catchpennies as Joice Heth, the Fejee Mermaid and the Woolly Horse to something more dignified.

The idea of engaging Jenny first came to him in October 1849. He figured the pros and cons over and over, and when he saw that prediction of his "cipherings" was always success, he authorized his agent—John Hall Wilton, an Englishman—to open negotiations with her. The final contract, signed at Lübeck on January 9, 1850, provided that

1. She would sing in 150 concerts or oratorios—"but

in no case to appear in opera"—in the United States and Havana, within eighteen months of her arrival in New York.

2. Barnum would pay her $1,000 for every performance; would furnish her a maid, a butler, and a secretary; would provide a carriage in each city; and would pay all expenses for herself and her staff, including a companion.

3. Barnum would pay all expenses, plus $25,000, to her musical director, Julius Benedict; and all expenses, plus $12,500, to Giovanni Belletti, a baritone who would reinforce her program.

4. Barnum would post the entire guarantee of $187,-500 with his London bankers before the party sailed from Europe.

Other provisions covered charity performances, the choice of songs, and a system of forfeits, but these four were the main ones.

As Jenny blotted her signature, she knew that she could now build her hospital, and that never again need she expose herself to the "vileness" of opera. She told Barnum later that she had had other offers to make an American tour. What had decided her in his favor was Wilton's first letter to her, on stationery headed with an engraving of Iranistan: "I said to myself, 'A gentleman who has been so successful in big business as to build such a palace cannot be a mere adventurer.' So I consented to an interview"—despite a rival showman's warning that Barnum wouldn't balk at putting her in a box and exhibiting her through the country at twenty-five cents a head.

Barnum was at his Museum in Philadelphia when, on February 19, he received a telegram from Wilton, newly arrived in New York: Jenny had signed and would reach America in September.

Not until then! If the contract were announced at once, its impact would be dissipated by September. Publicity would suffer; receipts, too. He wired Wilton to hold up the announcement, and started for New York by train next morning. Something went wrong; when he bought the New York papers at Princeton, they had the whole story. He decided to test the public's reaction at once. He told the conductor he had engaged Jenny Lind for a tour that fall.

"Jenny Lind?" the conductor asked. "Is she a dancer?"

Barnum's fears switched ends. Seven months, far from being too long to maintain interest in Jenny, perhaps was not long enough! His publicity machine went into high gear at once. Two days later appeared his first printed "letter" on the subject. It said in part:

I assure you that if I knew I should not make a farthing profit, I would ratify the engagement, so anxious am I that the United States should be visited by a lady whose vocal powers have never been approached by any other human being, and whose character is charity, simplicity, and goodness personified.

Miss Lind has numerous better offers . . . but she speaks

of this country and its institutions in the highest terms . . . , and as money is by no means the greatest inducement that can be laid before her, she is determined to visit us . . . She expressly reserves the right to give charitable concerts whenever she thinks proper.

Since her *début* in England, she has given to the poor . . . more than the whole amount which I have engaged to pay her, and the proceeds of her concerts for charitable purposes in Great Britain . . . have realized more than ten times that amount.

The single reference to her voice and the many to her generosity were shrewdly apportioned. Barnum's autobiography admits that "although I relied prominently upon Jenny Lind's reputation as a great musical *artiste,* I also took largely into my estimate of her success her extraordinary benevolence. Without this, I never would have dared make the engagement, as I felt sure there were multitudes who would be prompted to attend her concerts by this feeling alone."

His confidence was not shared by his bank. Its president told him, "Wall Street believes this venture will ruin you." As a result, he found it hard to muster the $187,500 bond. Even after liquidating much of his property, he was still $5,000 short. A clergyman lent it to him, and at last the path was clear for the enterprise "never before or since equalled in managerial annals."

As usual, he began with a crescendo drumfire in the press. He engaged a reporter to write two or three columns a week, ostensibly from London, about Jenny's popularity and philanthropies. *Jenny Lind*

Song Books and *Jenny Lind Annuals* went on sale. So did Jenny Lind gloves, bonnets, hats, shawls, mantillas, dolls, robes, chairs, sofas, pianos, "singing" teakettles and even sausages. Every shopwindow displayed her picture. As the day of her arrival drew close, Barnum pulled another string, with an announcement that "Jenny Lind having expressed a strong desire to sing at her first concert in New York a 'Welcome to America,' and Mr. Julius Benedict, the eminent composer, having volunteered to set such a composition to music, I hereby offer two hundred dollars for such a song."

The offer generated only mild publicity, but the award—to Bayard Taylor, of the *Tribune*—aroused such vociferous and prolonged resentment among the other 732 competitors that Barnum's purpose was amply served.

Shortly before Jenny sailed from Liverpool, she gave two farewell concerts. Barnum had arranged for them and had hired a critic to review them for a Liverpool paper, copies of which reached New York in time for reprinting just before her own arrival. So, when her ship, the *Atlantic*, finally docked at the foot of Canal Street, on September 1, 1850, all New York and most of America was in a fever to see the "prodigy of the century."

The crowd at the quayside was swelled to 30,000 by the lucky fact that September 1 fell on a Sunday. Barnum had not contrived that, of course, but the garlanded arches of welcome, the twined flags, the flowers, the carpet on the gangplank—"these were not produced by magic," he confessed, "and I do not know that I can reasonably find fault with those who suspected I had a hand in their erection." Conceivably, his hand also shoved, or at least bribed, the zealot who "fell" overboard in his loudly proclaimed eagerness to see Jenny Lind closer. Barnum did not confess this; he passed over it with one of his puns: instead of getting a view of the nightingale, all the poor man got was a cold duck.

Jenny threw a kiss to the American flag and tripped down the gangplank in a blue silk hat, a slate-colored dress, and a broadcloth cloak trimmed with velvet. The captain of the *Atlantic* escorted her to Barnum's carriage, through a crowd liberally laced with Museum employees, each equipped with a bouquet to be tossed as a "spontaneous tribute." Barnum climbed to the box, and they made their slow way to the Irving House, at Broadway and Chambers Street. Five thousand more people were waiting there, and within ten minutes another 15,000 had joined them. The crowd stayed for six hours, until 9 P.M., cheering and calling for its idol. At midnight, another crowd, even larger, gathered under her window, to hear her serenaded by 200 members of the New York Musical Fund Society. The cheers and calls became so clamorous that Barnum had to lead Jenny onto the balcony and let the crowd look at her, before the serenade could proceed.

Next day's *Tribune* gave her arrival four columns on its front page. All week the furor continued unabated. Mayor Caleb S. Woodhull awarded her the freedom of the city. She received a vote for lieutenant governor of Massachusetts. Songs, quadrilles, polkas and poems were dedicated to her. Visitors and presents packed her rooms. Barnum's only worry was lest society monopolize her and destroy the broader appeal of her simplicity and generosity, which he had been so diligently establishing.

The first concert was scheduled for Wednesday evening, September 11th. Tickets were sold by auction on the preceding Saturday and Monday. Although Saturday was rainy, more than 3,000 bidders showed up, and the first ticket went for $225 (the standard price was from $3 to a $7 top). The buyer was John N. Genin, a hatter whose shop was next door to the Museum. Barnum had urged him to bid the ticket in for its publicity value, and Genin never made a better purchase in his life. Every paper in the United States published his name, his business and his address; and he would sell 10,000 more hats in 1851 than in 1850.

Here appeared one of the most extraordinary offshoots of the Jenny Lind craze. An Iowa man who owned a Genin hat was able to knock it down second hand for $9.50—several times its original cost! In comparison, one can excuse, even approve, the ninnies who paid a shilling to the lucky gleaner of a glove Jenny dropped, for the privilege of kissing it.

The "Swedish Nightingale" Conquers America

WITH JENNY'S APPROVAL, BARNUM HAD CHOSEN CASTLE
Garden for her first series of concerts. It was New
York's largest auditorium, with a capacity of 10,000.
Barnum estimated that some 5,000 came to the open-
ing; others say 7,000; even the smaller figure repre-
sented a larger audience than she had ever faced before.
They began taking their places at 5 o'clock, three hours
before the overture. Each quarter of the auditorium
had its own color ticket, lamp and usher's costume.
Thanks to this ingenious system of Barnum's devising,
there was, unlike the dangerous "Jenny Lind crush" in
London, no disorder or confusion whatever.

The calm was deceptive. It lasted only until Jenny,

in a white dress, entered upstage, came forward with
Benedict, and curtsied toward a huge set piece of flowers spelling "Welcome Sweet Warbler." Then the audience rioted. (What might it have done if she hadn't
dissuaded Barnum from lowering her onstage with
wires and a belt, to suggest her angelic origin?)

That morning's *Herald* had gushed, "Jenny Lind is
the most popular woman in the world at this moment
—perhaps the most popular that ever was in it." "Popular" proved pallid; "idolized" would have been closer.
There were cheers and screams, and a wild flurry of
hats and handkerchiefs—louder and wilder and wilder
and louder. This was not mere popularity; it was
idolatry, hysteria, delirium. It infected even Jenny.
When she was allowed to sing at last, she stammered
and wavered, and nearly lost all control. But soon
she was her calm, sure self again, and she finished
"Casta Diva" to a storm of applause and bouquets.

The concert ended with Taylor's prize-winning
"Greeting to America." Jenny took three curtain calls,
then Barnum took one, at which he announced, to
more cheers, that Miss Lind was devoting her share—
$10,000—of the evening's receipts to a dozen charities
selected by herself, himself, and Mayor Woodhull. Actually, her share fell $1,500 short of $10,000; but
Barnum made up the deficit, and more, by an equal
division of receipts from the second concert as well.
These two were among the five most profitable concerts of the entire series. Barnum's generosity matched

Jenny's dollar for dollar, yet he kept it to himself, as he did the fact that whenever she gave one of her widely-publicized charity concerts, he always paid from his own pocket the cost of the hall, the orchestra and the advertising.

James Gordon Bennett's *Herald,* ignorant of the truth, began sniping at Barnum with such items as "Jenny Lind does all the generous acts, and Barnum perpetrates all the mean doings. He has not given a penny as yet for any charitable purpose, although he makes more out of Jenny's talents than Jenny does herself." Barnum let the falsehood pass unchallenged. Nor did he try to discourage circulation of a popular conundrum:

Q. Why will Jenny and Barnum never fall out?
A. Because she is always for-giving, and he is always for-getting.

Sometimes Jenny was represented as Barnum's accomplice, as when he was made to tell her,

They'll welcome you with speeches, and serenades
  and rockets
And you will touch their hearts, and I will tap their
  pockets;
And if between us both the public isn't skinned,
Why, my name isn't Barnum, nor your name Jenny
  Lind!

Barnum never sued. He never even protested. His philosophy was cynical but practical: "Say what you want about me so long as you say it loudly and spell my name correctly."

The reviews of Jenny's first concert were written in marshmallow whip and melted chocolate. Some of the more indigestible passages were "The song of the seraphim . . . Not Art; a manifestation of Nature . . . All feel her power, all go mad who see her, and they cannot explain the secret of her influence." Of a later concert, Dr. Lyman Abbott wrote in his Reminiscences, "It was impossible to doubt the Resurrection while she was singing 'I know that my Redeemer liveth.' She seemed a celestial witness."

Barnum assayed her power in other terms: "I think there were a hundred men in New York, the day after her first concert, who would have willingly paid me $200,000 for my contract. I received repeated offers for an eighth, a tenth, or a sixteenth, equivalent to that price. But mine had been the risk, and I was determined mine should be the triumph. So elated was I, . . . I do not think half a million of dollars would have tempted me to relinquish the enterprise."

After five concerts in New York, the troupe sailed for Boston, where fresh frenzies and fresh conquests awaited them. The F. Gleason press printed a welcoming broadside in gold ink and asked, "Are not all her deeds worthy to be thus chronicled?" The first ticket was auctioned to a local singer, Ossian F. Dodge, for $625, nearly three times what Genin had paid. At the next stop, Providence, a Col. William C. Ross bought the first ticket for $650 in gold.

Longfellow called on Jenny in Boston. So did Barnum's old friend Edward Everett, the former Minister to England and more recently President of Harvard. So did Daniel Webster, then Secretary of State. When he left, Jenny walked up and down her parlor, clasping her hands and repeating, "Ah, Mr. Barnum. That's a *man!* I have never before seen such a man!"

In Philadelphia, Barnum had to put Jenny's cloak and bonnet on her companion, Miss Ohmansson, and lead her onto the hotel balcony to satisfy the crowd below. In Baltimore, when Jenny herself appeared on the balcony and accidentally dropped her shawl, it was instantly shredded. In Washington, President Fillmore attended both her concerts with his family, his cabinet, and most of the members of Congress.

The troupe reached Charleston just before Christmas and stayed there ten days. Christmas night, Jenny gave them a party, with a tree and presents. Her ironic present to Barnum, a teetotaler, was a marble Bacchus. Wherever he lived thereafter, he kept it in his sitting room, along with a marble model of Tom Thumb's foot. She gave another party on New Year's Eve and insisted that Barnum dance a cotillion with her.

"I've never danced in my life!" he protested.

Jenny said, "All the better."

But Barnum had to write in his autobiography, "I

never saw her laugh more heartily than she did at my awkwardness. She said she would give me the credit of being the poorest dancer she ever saw!"

From Charleston they sailed to Havana. Two of Jenny's three concerts there had the smallest advance sale of all. The Habaneros thought the tickets too expensive; they called Barnum a "Yankee pirate" and hissed Jenny when she first came onstage. Then she began to sing. A few minutes later, the entire house was shouting "Encore!" and it held her for five curtain calls.

Barnum was waiting in the wings. He told her, "God bless you, Jenny! You've settled them!"

She threw her arms around his neck and sobbed, "Are you satisfied?"

Certainly the Habaneros were. They paid her their supreme tribute: they named a cigar for her.

The troupe spent a month in Havana. Jenny took a large house for them all, and there they had the happiest time of their tour. She bought a rubber ball and made Barnum play catch with her and mocked him for being "too fat and too lazy." One day Barnum had a visitor, a friend he hadn't seen for fourteen years: little Signor Vivalla. His left side was paralyzed now, so he could no longer balance plates, but he had trained a dog in a few tricks, and he was managing to live. Jenny heard his story and gave him $500, and Barnum arranged his passage back to Italy, but the brave little man died before he could sail.

New Orleans was the tour's halfway and high-water mark. The multitude that welcomed their ship made Jenny blench. Her month's vacation in Havana had intensified her mistrust of crowds; she told Barnum she couldn't face this one. Barnum's oldest daughter, Caroline, now nearly eighteen, was in the party. She veiled herself and took his arm, and while an assistant shouted, "Open the way for Mr. Barnum and Miss Lind, please!" they squeezed ashore to their carriage. Jenny and Miss Ohmansson joined them later, comfortably and unharassed.

Jenny gave more concerts to fatter receipts in New Orleans than in any city except New York. Such enthusiasm inspired Barnum to take the stage himself, for a lecture on temperance. He spoke for more than an hour, wittily and eloquently. Somebody in the audience asked, "How does alcohol affect us, externally or internally?"

"E-ternally," Barnum said.

He took the stage again on the side-wheeler that carried them up the Mississippi. After Jenny had sung for the passengers, Barnum told some jokes and did some conjuring tricks he had learned when he was barnstorming with old Aaron Turner, fifteen years before. He was good, for an amateur. His friend Joel Benton wrote that he "had many of the mimetic faculties of the actor, particularly a mobile face and versatility of expression. He was not a bad ventrilo quist, and in skilful acts of legerdemain he could have entertained audiences, with a little preliminary practice, night after night."

When they came to Nashville, he had another, and less happy, recollection of Aaron Turner and of all the other practical jokers of his youth. It was Turner who, once in Annapolis, pointed out Barnum as the Rev. Ephraim Avery, a notorious murderer; and a mob was preparing tar and feathers when he finally succeeded in identifying himself. Barnum never outgrew his adolescent admiration for these primitive pranks, and unluckily for the Jenny Lind troupe (and for his own reputation), they were in Nashville on his day of days, April 1st.

Barnum says he didn't start it: "I was considerably annoyed during the forenoon by the calls of members of the company who came to me under the belief that I had sent for them. After dinner I concluded to give them all a taste of 'April Fool'."

His "taste" was to send a score of fake telegrams: one, announcing to a prospective father that his wife had borne twins; others, to the singers and musicians, from opera managers offering them handsome salaries; still others, to the clerical staff, with propositions from banks and large companies. Most callous of all was the telegram to the general manager, LeGrand Smith, purporting to come from his father and informing him that his house had burned to the ground, with the rest of the village.

Many of the victims replied in good faith, and none

of them knew the sorry truth until they read it in next morning's newspaper.

It is consoling to learn that Smith soon evened the score. On the strength of a story he concocted, Barnum dreaded a highwayman's ambush all the way from Pittsburgh to Baltimore.

So the tour drew to its close. Barnum gave another temperance lecture at St. Louis. Business at Madison fell to $3,700—less than half the average; but at Cincinnati, the next stop, business was far above average. The first ticket had sold to a tailor for a thumping $575, and the clamorous crowd on the dock frightened Jenny, as at New Orleans. Cincinnati had heard of Barnum's ruse there with his daughter, so this time he escorted Jenny herself, under a thick veil, with Smith shouting, "That's no go! You can't pass your daughter off for Jenny Lind again!"

The crowd took it up: "You can't come it over us Buckeyes, Barnum! We intend to stay right here until you bring out Jenny Lind!"

They stayed there an hour before they discovered that he had "humbugged" them after all.

The last concert in Cincinnati was Jenny's seventy-sixth. She gave one in Wheeling, one in Pittsburgh, and fourteen in New York—her third series. Her third series in Philadelphia, too, had been booked, but she made only one appearance, then asked to terminate her contract. Although this meant a forfeit of $25,000 for not completing 150 concerts, and an additional forfeit of $7,000 for the seven concerts by which she fell short of completing 100, she paid it. And Barnum, with a feeling of "extravagant joy," went to Cape May for a week's rest, then home to Iranistan.

He was joyful because managing Jenny had become increasingly painful. Tension had built up over the nine months of their association. Her outbursts of temper were more and more frequent, and her demands for concessions (which Barnum granted without complaint) were more and more unreasonable. She was keyed up to them by her advisors, who were eager for one of themselves to be made her manager and to share the profits. They constantly poisoned her mind against Barnum. They defamed him as "nothing but a showman," unworthy to sponsor her celestial talents. They accused him of exploiting her, sweating her, turning her into a slave. Jenny came to believe it, so she and Barnum parted.

The gross recepits for her ninety-three concerts were $680,094.26, and her net receipts were $176,675.00, after paying the forfeits. Barnum did not publish the expenses, but if they amounted to some $350,000, as has been estimated, his net cash profit was approximately $215,000. His profit in prestige was incalculable.

Jenny continued to give concerts, but not with the same brilliant success. The novelty was wearing thin; the public's appetite was turning toward something more substantial than whipped cream and moonbeams.

The new management lacked Barnum's genius for promotion. Lastly, Jenny got engaged.

She had been engaged twice before, first to a Swedish opera singer and second to an English officer. Her new fiancé was a German pianist, Otto Goldschmidt, dull, literal-minded, and nine years younger than she. After their marriage in Boston in February 1852, she billed herself as "Madame Otto Goldschmidt (late Mlle. Jenny Lind)." Madame Goldschmidt gave her farewell American concert at Castle Garden on May 24th. Barnum, who had remained friendly, called at her dressing room to say goodbye. The *Herald* did not bother to review her, and when she sailed for England, where she spent the rest of her life, a crowd of only 2,000 saw her off. Marriage meant retirement; from then until her death in 1887, she sang scarcely at all. Goldschmidt lived until 1907.

More and More Schemes

BEFORE JENNY LIND'S ARRIVAL IN AMERICA, BARNUM
had embarked on another major enterprise. In equal
partnership with a veteran showman, Seth B. Howes,
and Charlie Stratton's father, Sherwood, he had chartered a ship and sent her to Ceylon, to replenish the
Museum's menagerie. She sailed in May, 1850 and returned to New York almost exactly a year later, during
Jenny's third series of concerts there. The prize of the
expedition was a herd of Singhalese elephants, the first
herd ever brought to America. Barnum had them harnessed in pairs to a chariot and paraded up Broadway
past the Irving House, so that Jenny could "review"
them from her balcony.

With the elephants as his star attraction, he organized Barnum's Great Asiatic Caravan, Museum and Menagerie, featuring an armless man, a lion tamer, a military band, General Tom Thumb, wax statues of all the Presidents, and other "WONDERFUL OBJECTS OF NATURE AND ART." At the end of a tour that lasted nearly four years and played to 5,824,000 customers, the three partners dismantled the Caravan and sold everything except one elephant. Barnum kept this for himself. It had given him an idea for an advertisement, one as simple and effective as any that ever occurred to him. He sent the elephant and its keeper to Bridgeport, and put them to plowing a six-acre field beside the New York & New Haven tracks. The keeper wore a turban, silk breeches and a yellow tunic, and made a point of always being busy when a passenger train went by.

Newspapers carried the story even in Europe. Tourists came by the hundreds. Barnum was nearly smothered by the letters that fell on him. His correspondents included state and county agricultural societies throughout America. The questions that most of them asked were these:

Is the elephant a profitable agricultural animal?
How much can an elephant plow in a day?
How much can he draw?
How much does he eat?
Will elephants make themselves generally useful on a farm?

What is the price of an elephant?

Where can elephants be purchased?

The tone of the letters was usually earnest, and Barnum became worried that the writers would buy elephants of their own. To discourage them, he printed a form reply in which he confessed that while his elephant was valuable as an advertisement, it was impractical as a farm animal—ate more than it earned, couldn't work in cold weather, and so on. He headed the form "Strictly Confidential," so that everybody receiving it could bask in his confidence. He kept the elephant for two months, then sold it to Van Amburgh's Menagerie.

Barnum might well have rested after his ordeal with Jenny Lind, but there was no corking up his energies. He engaged some musicians and sent them to give sixty concerts in California. He became president of the Pequonnock Bank in Bridgeport (and issued $5 bills bearing his picture and Jenny's). He wrote his autobiography, *The Life of P. T. Barnum, Written by Himself.* He resigned as president of the Fairfield County Agricultural Society in 1853, though the members refused to release him for another year. In 1854, he accepted the presidency of the Crystal Palace, a faltering international exposition in New York, but withdrew after three months, on the grounds that "the dead can not be raised."

Despite his manifold activities, all this time—as usual—the Museum was foremost in his thoughts. He was forever enlarging and improving it. In 1850, he added a collection of Chinese curiosities and engaged a Chinese "family" to supplement them—"the first time that a Chinese lady of consequence has ever been seen by the eyes of 'barbarians'." He staged a beauty contest and a baby show. He presented two Scottish fat boys who doubled as mind readers; and some child actors; and a Negro who claimed to know of a weed that could turn Negroes white. A contemporary poem, "Barnumopsis," celebrates

> *the marvellous Ethiope,*
> *Changing his skin by preternatural skill,*
> *Whom every setting sun's diurnal slope*
> *Leaves whiter than the last, and whitening still.*

The author lists the Museum's wonders, "monstrous, scaly, strange and queer," and urges the public,

> *Go lose thyself in those continuous halls*
> *Where strays the fond papa with son and daughter,*
> *And all that charms or startles or appals,*
> *Thou shalt behold, and for a single quarter!*

There was scarcely a freak anywhere, real or imaginary, from a four-legged chicken to a two-headed Mexican that was not brought to the Museum or at least offered it. One of Barnum's favorites was the Swiss bearded lady, Mme. Josephine Clofullia. He liked her because she lent herself to his special type of exploita-

tion, the controversy. It began with a spectator sum-
moning her to court as a humbug—"nothing more nor
less than a dressed-up man"—and demanding his
money back. Barnum testified to her authenticity; so
did her father and her husband; so did several doctors.
The case was dismissed, and Barnum and Madame
Clofullia were followed from the courtroom by a grati-
fyingly large crowd.

Some of the freaks offered him were less freaks of
nature than freaks of finance—mining stocks, patent
rights, and schemes "as wild and unfeasible," he wrote,
"as a railroad to the moon." One such was a company
to carry passengers to California by camels. Barnum
said he thought asses would be better for the purpose,
but he declined to be one of them. A soap manufacturer
wrote him,

PROVIDENCE, R. I.
Oct. 20th, 1853

BARNUM: I never saw you, nor you me, yet we
are not strangers. You have soaped the community,
and so have I. You are rich, I am not. I have a plan
to add half a million to your wealth, and many lau-
rels to your brow. I manufacture by far the best
soap ever known, as a million of gentlemen, and
three millions of God's greatest work, beautiful
women, will testify. I send you a sample to prove
the truth of my words. Try it, and when you find
that I state FACTS, . . . join me as an equal
partner, and we will thoroughly soap the American

Continent in three years, at a profit of a million dollars.

By doing this, sir, you will . . . aid in cleaning and purifying at least ten millions of your dirty fellow-citizens. It is a duty you owe to them and to yourself. Look at my portrait on the soap wrapper, and you will see the face of an honest man. Send me your check next week for $5,000, and the week after for $5,000 more, . . . and I will send you quarterly returns of profits. Come, old fellow, fork over, and no grumbling! . . .

My soap makes soft hands, and cures soft heads. It removes paint and grease, is unsurpassed for shaving, cures chaps on hands or face, and is death on foul teeth. It cures eruptions to a charm. I have no doubt that a sufficient quantity, properly applied, would cure the eruption of Vesuvius. . . .

PROFESSOR GARDNER,
Known as the New England Soap Man

Barnum withstood the professor's blandishments. His standard reply was, "If you should propose to get up a stock company for converting paving stones into diamonds, I would not join you." And yet he did join several flimsy promotions. He joined Commodore Vanderbilt in buying a steamship which soon sank. He last nearly $10,000 in a patent fire extinguisher. He lost $20,000 in a weekly newspaper. And presently he would lose Iranistan, the American Museum, and nearly everything else he owned.

At the Bottom of the Ladder

A FEW YEARS EARLIER, IN 1851, BARNUM AND A FRIEND
had bought 224 acres across the Pequonnock River
from Bridgeport. They wanted to build a model town
there, with parks, trees, busy factories and neat houses.
One of the businesses they hoped to attract was the
Jerome Clock Company of New Haven, which employed more than 700 workmen and was the largest
and most famous clock manufactory in America. Jerome
clocks were sold all over the world, even in China,
where the natives sometimes took out the movements
and used the cases as shrines—"thus proving," said
Barnum, "that faith was possible without 'works'."
Early in 1855, he discussed the move with officers of
the company, who told him that although it had a
capital of $400,000 and a surplus of $187,000, it needed

$110,000 more to tide it over a dull season. If Barnum would endorse notes for this amount, they would transfer to East Bridgeport as soon as convenient.

Barnum made no bones about admitting that East Bridgeport was his hobby, his pet. A naïve businessman at best, and now besotted with his grandiose city-building plan, he signed notes right and left. "Never," he said afterwards, "did I feel stronger in my worldly prosperity than in September, 1855." Three months later, he suddenly discovered that his notes totaled more than half a million dollars. What awakened him to his folly was a report, shocking but true, that Jerome Clock had gone into bankruptcy and would pay only fifteen cents on the dollar. Hurriedly, Barnum met all his personal debts, amounting to some $40,000, then he went into bankruptcy, too.

The echoes of his crash flew far and wide. They were lent wings by the fact that his recently-published autobiography shamelessly admitted his humbugs. He had been especially audacious in revealing that a great many editors had been his dupes and confederates, and some of these same editors now revenged themselves. Here is how his old arch enemy, James Gordon Bennett of the *Herald,* fell upon him:

The author of that book glorifying himself as a millionaire from the arts and appliances of obtaining money upon false pretenses is . . . completely crushed out. All the profits of all his Fejee Mermaids, all his woolly horses, Greenland whales, Joice Heths, negroes turning white, Tom Thumbs, and monsters and impostures of all kinds, including the reported $70,000 received by the copyright of that book, are all swept away, Hindoo palace, elephants, and all, by the late invincible showman's remorseless assignees. It is a case eminently adapted to "point a moral or adorn a tale."

But such vindictiveness was exceptional. Most people not only were sympathetic, but were eager to prove it. The Mayor of Bridgeport presided over a mass meeting which passed resolutions in Barnum's behalf, and a group of Bridgeport citizens offered to lend him $50,000. A thousand leading New Yorkers, including Commodore Vanderbilt, signed an open letter urging him to accept a series of benefits for his family. Friends pressed upon him checks for $500 and more. His daughter, Helen, then fifteen, offered to leave her expensive boarding school and give piano lessons. Her letter moved him to tears. So did a letter from Tom Thumb:

> JONES' HOTEL, PHILADELPHIA
> *May 12, 1856*
>
> MY DEAR MR. BARNUM:
>
> I understand your friends (and that means "all creation") intend to get up some benefits for your family. Now, my dear sir, just be good enough to remember that I belong to that mighty crowd, and I must have a finger (or at least a "thumb") in that pie. I have just started out on my western tour, and have my carriage, ponies and assistants all here, but I am ready to go on to New York and remain at Mrs. Barnum's service as long as I, in

my small way, can be useful. Put me into any "heavy" work, if you like. Perhaps I cannot lift as much as some other folks, but I can draw a tremendous load. I drew two hundred tons at a single pull today, embracing two thousand persons . . . Hoping that you will be able to fix up a lot of magnets that will attract all New York, and volunteering to sit on any part of the loadstone, I am, as ever, your little but sympathizing friend,

GEN. TOM THUMB.

Barnum watched his accounts and properties melt away. When a bank foreclosed its mortgage on Iranistan, the "Hindoo Palace," Barnum said, "The name was prophetic: 'I ran, I stand'; I ran into a scrape and I will stand the burden of it."

"At the age of forty-six," he wrote in the next edition of his autobiography, "after the acquisition and loss of a handsome fortune, I was once more nearly at the bottom of the ladder and was about to begin the world again. The situation was disheartening, but I had energy, experience, health and hope."

He failed to include in this list of assets certain others which were rather more readily negotiable. For instance, although he had sold the Museum collection the summer before, he had kept the lease of the building and had turned it over to Charity, his wife, along with "much valuable property." This was done not to evade his debts, but in anticipation of retirement. The lease was worth $19,000 a year and had twenty-two years to run, so Barnum could say—and did—"I am not only a proper 'subject of charity,' but 'without Charity I am nothing.' "

If starvation was not among his liveliest hobgoblins, lawyers were. They deviled him relentlessly. They delighted, he says, in putting him through "a course of sprouts." Day after day, lawyer after lawyer representing creditor after creditor would hale him into court and drag him over ground already as thoroughly plowed as his six-acre field by the railroad tracks. Barnum's patience sometimes snapped.

One lawyer demanded to know his business.

"Attending bar."

"Attending bar! Don't you profess to be a temperance man? Where do you attend bar, and for whom?"

Barnum answered, "I attend the bar of this court nearly every day, for the benefit of two-penny, would-be lawyers and their greedy clients!"

But finally the torment was over, and he was released, to go home and lick his wounds. The deepest and slowest to heal was inflicted when he learned that the clock factory would not transfer to his beloved East Bridgeport after all.

"Home" was now a rented house in New York, on Eighth Street, off Sixth Avenue. Here he and his family took in boarders until the late spring, when Charity's poor health required a move to the seaside. Barnum found them rooms at a farmhouse near Quogue, Long

Island; and strolling along the beach there one summer morning, he found something else: a young black whale, twelve feet long, stranded, but still firm and fresh. The bankrupt forgot his lawsuits; the showman remembered his show. He quickly arranged for icing the whale and shipping it to the Museum, and the new owners paid him enough for it to meet his family's board for the whole season.

The tide that had washed the whale ashore was symbolic of the tide in Barnum's affairs, already flooding again. A big sewing-machine company's move to East Bridgeport made his faith soar anew. He borrowed $5,000 and bought back some of his real estate, and these lots eventually repaid him more than he had lost in the Jerome disaster. His theory of investment was, "Growing trees, money at interest, and rapidly rising real estate, work for their owners all night as well as all day, Sundays included, and when the proprietors are asleep or away."

"Away" was the key word for Barnum. He was born on a Thursday, and his whole life was testimony to the old jingle that says, "Thursday's child has far to go." Now, as his dark year, 1856, drew to a close, he planned another trip. It would be one of his longest, and his traveling companion would be one of his favorites. He was accepting the offer of his "little but sympathizing friend." Nearly ten years had passed since their last tour together—years that had not left Charlie unmarked. He had added two inches and several pounds. Those three-inch shoes had begun to cramp him, so he had taken them off for the last time. He had stopped concealing his real age, eighteen, and as became a rich young sportsman, had bought a racing yacht. Moreover, his father had died in 1855, so he was now head of the Stratton family.

Barnum's plan for the General and himself had sprung from his awareness that the burning topic of the day was slavery. *Uncle Tom's Cabin*, by Harriet Beecher Stowe, had been published in 1852 and now, four years later, was still a runaway best seller. "Tom shows," a crudely dramatized version of the novel, were playing in every hamlet in the land. The cause of abolition was coming to a crisis in the Dred Scott Case, being tried before the Supreme Court, and Mrs. Stowe met it with another slavery novel, *Dred, A Tale of the Great Dismal Swamp*. This, too, was partly dramatized, in a skit built around Tom Tit, a comic Negro boy. So, Mrs. Stowe having hitched herself to a controversial issue, Barnum—ever quick to capitalize on a controversy—hitched himself to Mrs. Stowe. Since slavery was being debated abroad almost as furiously as at home, he proposed to tour Europe with two different troupes centering around three different Toms. One troupe would feature Tom Thumb in his usual popular repertory, spiced with the new role of Tom Tit. The other would be a Tom show, featuring young Cordelia Howard* as Eva, her father as St. Clair and her mother as Topsy.

They all sailed from New York early in 1857. Ordinarily, Barnum arrived and departed to drums and trumpets. This time he was almost furtive. Fearful of having his money attached, he crept aboard the ship with empty pockets, and was slipped a purse by a friend who returned in the pilot boat.

* Aged 4½, she had created the role at the Troy Museum on September 27, 1852. Lincoln saw her play it in Washington. She died in 1941, aged ninety-three.

The Art of Money-Getting

THE TOUR OF ENGLAND WAS HAPPY, FRIENDLY AND PROS-
perous as before. The Brighton *Guardian* welcomed
"His Yankee Diminutiveness General Tom Thumb,
Representative (very) Extraordinary of the Stars and
Stripes . . . still the same rollicking, jolly little blade."
Emotional audiences everywhere wept at Eva, laughed
at Topsy, and hissed at Simon Legree:

> Legree he sported a brass-buttoned coat,
> A snake-skin necktie, a blood-red shirt.
> Legree he had a beard like a goat,
> And a thick hairy neck, and eyes like dirt.

From England, Barnum and his troupe went to Scotland, Ireland and Wales, then across to Paris and up
into Germany. Barnum, the former lottery agent, was

shocked (or pretended to be) by the reckless gambling at Baden-Baden and did his best to discourage it by raising the price of tickets to his shows. At Wiesbaden, the General added William III, King of Holland, to the lost list of his royal admirers; but disappointingly, there is no record of a gorgeous present in what the General had come to regard as a royal tradition.

Holland itself, on the other hand, was anything but a disappointment. It gave Barnum "more genuine satisfaction" than any other country he had ever visited, except Great Britain. The dykes were "monuments of the industry of the whole generation of human beavers." He was impressed by the natives' neatness and "extraordinary cleanliness." Indeed, his autobiography labors the point so heavily that readers finally suspect they are being set up for a pun. And they are. "There is a constant exercise of brooms, pails, floor-brushes, and mops all over Holland," Barnum wrote—so much so that in some places "the only trees are scrub-oaks."

Charity and their two younger daughters, Helen and Pauline, arrived in London that summer. Barnum had hardly settled them in a modest house when, in August, business drew him back to America. His family followed a month later, and in October Helen was married. The eldest daughter, Caroline, had been married in 1852. Iranistan caught fire on her wedding day and had barely been saved. Two months after Helen's wedding, it caught fire again. This time it burned to the ground. Some of the furnishings were saved, but the

$28,000 insurance policy came nowhere near covering the loss.

Ever since Barnum's bankruptcy, his "beautiful Iranistan" had stood empty. His creditors offered to let him use it until a purchaser appeared, and workmen had started refurbishing it for his return. One of them, rumor said, had left his pipe on a cushion in the Dome Room. Whatever the cause, up in flames and down in ashes went what would have been a uniquely flamboyant monument to a uniquely flamboyant man. Barnum did not exaggerate when he called it "a public calamity." The property was sold for $50,000 to Elias Howe, Jr., the inventor of the sewing machine. Howe intended erecting another mansion there, but he died first. (The site is now occupied by several houses, an auditorium and a filling station.)

Barnum sent Charity and Pauline to live with Caroline and her husband, and returned to England soon after the New Year, 1858. The General had waited for him, before starting another swing around the circuit. Both were old hands at it by now; the famous act required only cursory attention. Accordingly, Barnum entrusted the end of the tour to agents and applied himself to a new enterprise: lecturing.

His subject, suggested by his friends, was "The Art of Money-Getting." He protested that—on his record— he was better qualified to discuss the art of money-losing, but they pointed out that he could not have lost it if he had **not** first had it. He engaged St. James' Hall and thoroughly advertised his début for December 29. Every one of the 3,000 seats was filled. The price of admission bought an address which now seems little more than a mixture of such platitudes and proverbs as:

Spend less than you earn, but beware of false economy; don't be like "the man who bought a penny herring for his family's dinner and then hired a coach-and-four to take it home."

Vanity is dangerous; "many persons become ruined in their ridiculous attempts to keep up appearances and make a 'sensation.'"

"The foundation of success in life is good health; get plenty of fresh air and never, never use tobacco or alcohol."

The rest was divided into sections headed, Don't mistake your vocation; Select the right location; Avoid debt; Persevere; Whatever you do, do with all your might; Depend upon your own personal exertions; Use the best tools; and so on.

Each section was illustrated with anecdotes and garnished with maxims. A twentieth-century audience would have nodded and dozed after the first few minutes, but the audience of a century ago was enthralled, judging from the next day's reviews.

Other audiences agreed. Within ten months, Barnum revealed the art of money-getting more than 100 times —an average of once every three days. A London publisher offered him $6,000 for the copyright, but Barnum declined. He wanted to print the lecture in the next edition of his autobiography, as well as deliver it in America. He records that he lectured more than 700 times in all, to a total audience of 1,300,000.

When he reached New York late in 1859, his receipts from Tom Thumb, the Tom show, and his English lectures, plus his commission on novelties bought for the Museum, had piled so high that he was able to pay off all but the last $20,000 of his clock company debts. Better yet, he bought back the Museum. The agreement was signed on St. Patrick's Day, 1860, possession to be given a week later. The new management had offered the same attractions as Barnum's, but it had not baited them with Barnum's special allure. This allure Barnum now prepared to provide afresh. He blazoned New York with flags, posters and banners announcing "Barnum's on his feet again!" On opening night, he took the stage of the Moral Lecture Room before a capacity audience, and rehearsed the story of his recent past:

"After nearly five years of hard struggle to keep my head above water, I have touched bottom at last, and here, tonight, I am happy to announce that I have waded ashore."

Among the novelties he had sent on from Europe was the Lucasie family, whom he had engaged in Holland. They were albinos, so when Barnum proclaimed their "pure white skin, silken white hair and pink eyes," he was merely straining the frame of truth, but he broke it entirely when he added, "——though born of perfectly BLACK PARENTS!!" He could never let well enough alone. Tom Thumb had to be artificially aged to eleven. The Woolly Horse had to be Colonel Frémont's. The Lucasies had to have black parents and come from Madagascar. Not that the public cared; attendance at the Museum doubled.

Barnum wrote of his first year (second term) as owner of the Museum, "Curiosities began to pour into the halls." One of the most famous and most enduring was Zip, the What-is-it?, also known as the Man Monkey and the Missing Link. Zip was a Negro boy whose cone-shaped skull tapered to a crown no larger than a baseball. He shaved his head daily but let a top-knot grow, until he looked like a sea anemone. His skin was grotesquely wrinkled. He communicated by grimaces and grunts. If anyone handed him a cigar, he ate it.

His nickname is said to have been bestowed by Charles Dickens, who, on seeing him for the first time, asked, "What is it?" Barnum cried, "That's what it is: a What-is-it!" This may be fancy, but it is a fact that although three generations of circus fans knew Zip well, few fans knew that his was a painstaking imposture. His real name was William H. Jackson. His skull was deformed, but his brain was not; he was intelligent, popular and warm-hearted. Almost his last words, before his death at eighty-odd in 1926, were these, to his sister: "Well, we fooled 'em a long time, didn't we?"

Eighteen sixty-one was Barnum's aquatic year. All his interest and activity were focused on the water. He sent a fishing smack to Bermuda to bring back a collection of tropical fish. He bought out the Aquarial Gardens in Boston and moved its best specimens to New York. He enlisted the attention of all freshwater fishermen by his standing offer of $100 for a live brook trout weighing four pounds or more. He arranged for the capture of some white whales in the St. Lawrence River and exhibited them in a tank twenty-four feet square. After three pairs of whales had died, he turned the tanks over to the first hippopotamus ever seen in America.

FROM THE RIVER NILE IN EGYPT,
THE GREAT BEHEMOTH OF THE SCRIPTURES,
AND THE MARVEL OF THE ANIMAL KINGDOM.

The advertisement continued, in Barnum's best vein, "AMPHIBIOUS ANIMAL . . . wild and ferocious . . . FRIGHTFUL ANTAGONIST . . . gigantic proportions and herculean strength . . . frequently destroying whole boat-loads of men and their boats, crushing with their huge jaws everything that comes in their way . . . a native ARABIAN KEEPER, SALAAMA . . . the only man who can control or exhibit his Hippopotamiship, is in constant attendance."

An exception to 1861's aquatic creatures was the famous cherry-colored cat. A farmer described it in exactly those words and offered it sight unseen to Barnum's manager, John Greenwood, with an affidavit that it was alive, healthy and not dyed. Greenwood paid out $25 and received an ordinary black cat. It was obviously alive, evidently healthy and, as the farmer hastened to point out, the color of *black* cherries. Barnum, delighted, gave it an engraved collar and introduced it among "The Happy Family."

Magnetic as were these attractions, winter brought Barnum one that would take its place among his dozen greatest of all time. This was George Washington Morrison Nutt of Manchester, New Hampshire. He was eighteen years old, handsome and cocky—and he was twenty-nine inches tall and weighed twenty-four pounds. His juicy contract with Barnum gave him $10,000 a year for three years, plus expenses for himself and a companion. The newspapers immediately termed him "the $30,000 Nutt," but Barnum, still in his aquatic phase, "commissioned" him commodore, and as "Commodore Nutt" he is known to circus history. His title required a naval uniform, and his family name suggested a carriage like half an English walnut shell. There were ponies to match, of course, with gold-mounted harness, and a coachman and footman in livery.

Barnum's standard technique in publicizing midgets was to associate them with the highest and mightiest in the land. His formula now ran, "As Queen Victoria was to General Tom Thumb, President Lincoln will be to Commodore Nutt." Accordingly, he took the Commodore to the White House, where the President received them and introduced them to his Cabinet. As they left, Lincoln leaned far down to shake the midget's little hand and said, "Commodore, permit me to give you a parting word of advice. When you are in command of your fleet, if you find yourself in danger of being taken prisoner, I advise you to wade ashore."

The Commodore craned his neck to see Lincoln's whole length: "I guess, Mr. President, you could do that better than I could."

The physical resemblance between the Commodore and the General was primarily one of feature; their statures were hardly alike at all. The General, six years older than the Commodore, was six inches taller now and almost twice as heavy. But facially, except for the General's mustache, they might have been twins. The first time the Commodore visited Barnum in Bridgeport, he was greeted everywhere with "Hi, Charlie! Welcome home!", even by friends of the General's since his infancy. The General's own sister, Mary Elizabeth, said that the Commodore looked so much like her brother, she was "loath to let him go." Many people stubbornly maintained that it was another of Barnum's humbugs: the Commodore actually *was* the General.

None of this escaped Barnum's attention, and no one had to point out the opportunity to turn the controversy into cash, by bringing the two midgets together. New York had not seen the General for six years. At the moment, he was touring the West. Barnum wrote him that his appearance with the Commodore would be a "natural," and the General agreed. When he returned, "The Two Smallest Men and Greatest Curiosities Living," their act supported by Anna Swan of Nova Scotia —seventeen years old, seven feet eleven inches tall, 413 pounds—began a successful four-weeks' run in mid-August.

Meanwhile, Barnum had quietly engaged still another midget, a young woman. The General knew nothing about her; neither did the Commodore. Barnum had smuggled her down to New York and into the St. Nicholas Hotel, where he could polish her wardrobe and her demeanor in private, for her surprise opening at the Museum that fall.

She was Mercy Lavinia Warren Bump, a school teacher from Middleboro, Massachusetts—a New Englander like the General and the Commodore. Their vital statistics were:

	Age	Height	Weight
Mercy Lavinia	21	32	29
The General	24	35	47
The Commodore	18	29	24

Mercy Lavinia's younger sister, Minnie, was also a midget; her two older sisters and her four brothers were of normal size. On their mother's side, they traced their ancestry through Richard Warren of the *Mayflower* to William, Earl of Warren, and his wife

Gruneda, daughter of William the Conqueror. Mercy Lavinia herself was a Colonial Dame and a Daughter of the American Revolution. Barnum did not change her name or prefix a military title, as with his other midgets. He merely shortened it, and Mercy Lavinia Warren Bump became Lavinia Warren.

14

The Marriage of the Midgets

THE GENERAL AND THE COMMODORE ENDED THEIR RUN, and the General retired to his yacht and his fast horses, leaving the Commodore to carry on at the Museum. It was then that Lavinia made her début. She was chic and charming; she had a pretty pink and white complexion; and—possibly because she had been born on Hallowe'en—she bewitched the Commodore until his backbone twanged like a harpstring. Inevitably, they were much in one another's company, and inevitably the Commodore read reciprocated interest into Lavinia's casual courtesies, although she—a woman of the world who had entertained Astors and Vanderbilts in her hotel suite, not to mention such heroes as Generals McClellan and Burnside—could regard him as no more than "a nice little boy." Worse, his hopes were falsely encouraged when, at Barnum's thoughtless suggestion, she gave him a diamond and emerald ring which she had received from Barnum and had found too large. The Commodore looked on it as a love-token, a positive response, and—to Lavinia's helpless embarrassment— pressed his suit with renewed ardor.

That was the situation when the General came down from Bridgeport one autumn day and dropped in at the Museum. Lavinia was there. The general met her, chatted a moment and took his leave. Immediately he asked Barnum for a private interview, and as soon as they were alone, he blurted out, "That's the most charming little lady I ever saw! I believe she was created on purpose to be my wife. You've always been a friend of mine. Say a good word for me to her! I've got plenty of money. I want to marry and settle down in life, and I really feel as if I must marry that young lady!"

A pun popped into Barnum's head, and for him to think of one was to speak it. "Lavinia is engaged already," he said gravely.

"To whom? Commodore Nutt?"

"No, General. To me."

The General laughed with relief. That was all he needed to know. Forthwith his cocked hat was in the ring. To the neglect of his playthings in Bridgeport, he began spending more and more time in New York, at the Museum, close to Lavinia. The Commodore could only grind his teeth in rage; he had to work for a living and make regular appearances onstage, whereas the General was a man of leisure. The Commodore muttered of pistols and bowie knives and his skill at boxing, but the General was deaf to all warnings. Even when the Commodore could no longer contain the pressure of his emotions and attacked him in their dressing room, it served only to steel the General's purpose. But before he could utter the proposal to which he was resolved, his mother's consent was necessary. He therefore asked Barnum to invite Lavinia to Bridgeport for the weekend, so that Cynthia Stratton could meet her. Barnum did so, but tactlessly issued his invitation in the presence of the Commodore, who at once said he would like to go too. Barnum protested that the Museum could not spare both its stars at the same time, but he finally agreed to let the Commodore off for the 8 o'clock train on Saturday evening. Barnum and Lavinia were traveling up that morning.

The Barnums and their youngest daughter, Pauline, were living at Lindencroft, their second residence in Bridgeport. He had built it two years before, about 500 yards west of the Iranistan property, and had named it for Jenny Lind. Though neither so bizarre nor so huge as Iranistan, Lindencroft was far from bleak. Barnum had stocked it with "fountains, shrubbery, statuary and all that could adorn it." Here is where he had invited Lavinia—where, as he probably remarked, Charity would meet with Mercy.

The General was waiting at the Bridgeport station

in his smartest carriage. (The coachman wore a broad velvet ribbon, Barnum noticed, and a new silver buckle on his hat.) Lavinia rested for half an hour at Lindencroft, then went driving with the General, who did not fail to point out the many properties in his real estate portfolio and Barnum's. She was duly impressed. She told Barnum later, "It seems as if you and Tom Thumb own about all Bridgeport!"

Lindencroft dined at five. The General and his mother were prompt. The conversation was gay, and when Mrs. Stratton left at seven—the General was spending the night—she expressed her sincere pleasure at meeting Lavinia. As the Commodore would not arrive until eleven, Barnum redeemed his previous tactlessness by retiring with Charity, leaving Lavinia and the General alone, playing backgammon.

But not so alone as they believed. "A couple of mischievous young ladies" (Barnum identifies them only thus, but one of them was almost certainly his daughter) were also staying at Lindencroft. Unknown to either the host or the other guests, they crouched on the dark stairs, in full view and earshot of the backgammon game. What follows they reported to Barnum, who wrote it down "with the sanction of those most interested."

As soon as quiet fell over the house, the General let the backgammon game flag. He must have rated his wealth as his strongest selling point, because he opened his campaign by showing Lavinia an insurance policy and explaining its advantages.

Lavinia said only, "Very nice."

He hitched his chair a little closer. "So you're going to Europe soon?" The businessman had established himself; now it was the turn of the citizen of the world.

"Yes, Mr. Barnum intends to take me over in a couple of months."

"You'll find it very pleasant. I've been there twice. In fact, I've spent six years abroad, and I like the old countries very much."

Lavinia said, "I hope I'll like the trip and I expect I shall. Mr. Barnum says I'll visit all the principal cities, and no doubt I'll be invited to appear before the Queen of England, the Emperor and Empress of France, the King of Prussia, the Emperor of Austria, and at the courts of any other countries we may visit. Oh, I'll like that! It'll be so new to me!"

"Yes, it'll be very interesting indeed. I've visited most of the crowned heads," the General said smugly. "I wish I was going over. I know all about the different countries and could explain them all to you."

"That would be very nice."

He hitched his chair closer still. "Do you think so?"

Lavinia said calmly, "It would be pleasant to have some person along who could answer all my foolish questions."

The citizen of the world melted into the lover, and the lover slipped his arm behind her. "Would you *really* like to have me go?"

"Of course I would!"

He hugged her tightly and whispered, "Don't you think it would be pleasanter if we went as man and wife?"

Lavinia declared that he must be joking; the General said he had never been more serious. Lavinia wondered why the Commodore didn't come; the General said that he himself wasn't at all anxious. Lavinia protested that this was so sudden; the General countered that they were long and well-acquainted. Lavinia said that her mother didn't like his moustache; the General swore he would cut it off and, if need be, his ears too. Lavinia was looking for another objection when the General kissed her, and that was that.

A few minutes later, a carriage drove up and in strode the Commodore. "*You* here, General?" he asked coldly.

Lavinia broke in, "Yes, Mr. Barnum asked him to stay. We were waiting for you."

"Where's Mr. Barnum?"

"He's gone to bed," the General said.

"Which room does he sleep in?"

They told him, and the Commodore dashed upstairs so fast that the two young eavesdroppers barely had time to duck out of sight. Barnum was in bed, reading.

The Commodore wasted no time on civilities. He demanded, "Does Tom Thumb *board* here?"

"No," Barnum told him, "Tom Thumb does *not* board here. I invited him to stop overnight. Don't be foolish. Go to bed!"

The Commodore had hardly stumped out, scowling, when the General scampered in, beaming. He grabbed Barnum's hand and whispered, "We're engaged, Mr. Barnum! We're engaged! We're *engaged!*" He bounced up and down in his excitement, but finally composed himself enough to warn Barnum, "Please don't say a word! I had to tell *you,* of course, but 'mum's the word!' "

The following Wednesday, Barnum and the two fiancés met in New York. The General had written Lavinia's mother for her consent and was awaiting his friend George Wells, who had carried the letter to Middleboro. He was so confident of Mrs. Bump's answer that he remarked to Barnum, "I want somebody to tell the Commodore."

Barnum said, "Do it yourself, General."

"I wouldn't dare," the General said. "He might knock me down!"

Lavinia said, "*I'll* do it."

Her news was a cruel blow to the Commodore. He blanched and turned away, just managing to choke out, "I hope you may be happy."

His more immediate hope was that Mrs. Bump

would be outraged and obstinate. But Wells was all smiles when he returned next day, and there was nothing left for the Commodore but to bite the bullet. True, Mrs. Bump had indeed objected at first, but Wells convinced her that it was a genuine love match and not a scheme of Barnum's. Her fears did Barnum an injustice. He promised a "genteel and graceful" wedding and he kept his promise, although he could have sold invitations for sixty dollars apiece. Only once did he waver. News of the engagement catapulted Museum receipts to such a height—$3,000 a day—that he offered the General $15,000 to postpone the wedding for a month.

The General was indignant. "No, sir! Not for *fifty* thousand!"

Lavinia cried, "Good for you, Charlie! Only, you should have said, 'Not for a *hundred* thousand!'"

The wedding took place in Grace Church, New York City, at noon on February 10, 1863. The maid-of-honor was Lavinia's midget sister, Minnie, and the best man was Commodore Nutt. He had declined the honor when Barnum offered it, but had later accepted it from the General.

"It wasn't your place to ask me," he explained to Barnum stiffly. "When the proper person did, I said I would."

The two thousand guests included generals, governors, members of Congress, other celebrities and "the social élite" of New York. The bride wore tulle, flounced with lace that cost $50 a yard—a present from Barnum—and carried a bouquet of roses and camellias. Her diamond earrings, necklace and bracelet were from the groom. Three clergymen officiated. As soon as the benediction had been pronounced, the General "saluted his wife with an honest kiss, the last of nearly three million pressed in public upon the lips of his lady admirers."

Barnum gave the reception at the Metropolitan Hotel. While Lavinia cut a cake that weighed twice as much as herself, the guests goggled at the presents. President and Mrs. Lincoln sent a set of Chinese fire screens "richly inlaid with gold, silver and pearl." Vanderbilts, Astors, Belmonts and Bennetts sent "very chaste souvenirs" of jewelry, silver and porcelain. Black and Ball, the diamond merchants, sent Lavinia a diamond watch; Gunther, the furrier, an ermine cape; Tiffany, a silver chariot. Various manufacturers sent their wares in miniature: furniture, tea services, a silver-plated sewing machine, a billiard table, a baby baby-grand. Commodore Nutt gave them a diamond ring—too small, the jealous General noted, for anyone's finger but Lavinia's smallest. Barnum gave them a tortoise-shell casket; press a button, and a tiny mechanical bird with real feathers popped out and warbled.

Barnum also gave Lavinia "an international gown," to be worn when she met royalty on her European tour. It was made of thin silk that shaded from silver to amber, and the panels of the skirt, connected by marabou feathers and lace, displayed seven national emblems: "in front, Growing Corn for America; on the right, a Rose for England; on the left, a Laurel for France; on other breadths, an Acorn in Oak Leaves for Germany, a Shamrock for Ireland, a Thistle for Scotland, and a Vine with Clusters of Grapes for Italy."

The climax of the honeymoon trip was a reception at the White House, during which Lincoln asked, "Well, General, what is your opinion of the war, as a military man?"

And the General replied, "My opinion is that my friend Barnum would settle the whole affair in a month!"

The White House served Barnum's ends again the following year, when he intercepted a party of ten Indian Chiefs en route to call on the President, and by a bribe to their interpreter sidetracked them to the Museum. The chiefs' innocent belief that they were Barnum's honored guests, and that the daily crowds were come to do them homage, was encouraged by the ceremony with which he introduced them from the platform. When, for instance, he presented Yellow Bear, chief of the Kiowas, nothing in Barnum's respectful manner suggested a translation of what he was saying: "Here is probably the meanest black-hearted rascal in the Far West, a lying, thieving, treacherous, murderous monster!" In much the same manner he introduced White Bull of the Apaches, Hand-in-the-Water of the Cheyennes, and all the rest. After a week, one of the chiefs discovered Barnum's trick and they all swept off to Washington, grunting dudgeon.

15

Haunted by the Number 13

WHEN THE CIVIL WAR BEGAN IN APRIL, 1861, BARNUM was fifty, too old for military service, but he hired four substitutes, as was permissible then, and gave generously to the Union cause. He sincerely hated slavery. The main reason he ran (as a Republican) for the Connecticut General Assembly in 1865 was that "it would be an honor to be permitted to vote for the then proposed amendment to abolish slavery forever from the land." He was elected and was speaking from the floor on July 13 when he received a telegram from the assistant manager of the American Museum, his daughter Helen's husband, Samuel H. Hurd: The Museum was on fire and was threatened with to- tal destruction. According to a Hartford newspaper, "Without the slightest evidence of agitation, Barnum laid the telegram upon his desk and finished his speech. When he went next day to New York he saw only a pile of black, smouldering ruins."

One fire had broken out the year before, but watchmen had doused it quickly. Now, a bear, a few monkeys, some birds and the educated seal were all that remained of a collection which had needed twenty-five years to amass and had featured many irreplaceable items, including relics of the Revolution. Losses were $400,000; insurance was $40,000.

Horace Greeley told Barnum, "Accept this fire as a notice to quit, and go a-fishing."

Barnum's first impulse was to obey, but two other considerations triumphed: 150 employees would be out of work, and New York City needed a good museum. (A possible third consideration was that the museum business was profitable.) He leased the Chinese Museum buildings at Broadway and Prince Streets, sent agents to scour the world for fresh curiosities, bought and combined several small collections, and opened "Barnum's New American Museum" exactly four months after the disaster to the old one.

Happily, the $400,000 loss did not include his long and enormously valuable lease on the property. This he now sold for a thumping $200,000 to James Gordon Bennett, the newspaper publisher, who put an additional $500,000 into buying the lot and the shell of the building, intending to erect a more stately mansion for his *Herald*. As his commitments mounted,

Bennett became frightened and tried to make Barnum cancel the deal, and when Barnum refused, Bennett rejected all advertising for the new Museum. His tactics proved as costly as they were hotheaded. Barnum belonged to the Producing Managers' Association, and when the other members heard his grievance, they voted unanimously to deny Bennett their own advertising and job printing. Not for two years did they call off their boycott. After Bennett's death in 1872, his equally hotheaded son tried to rekindle the old feud, but Barnum cooled him down with, "Young man, I knew you when you rode the hobby-horse which I bought for Tom Thumb."

These years, the latter 1860's, were busy ones for Barnum. He was re-elected to the Legislature in '66 and was nominated for Congress in '67, but lost in a Democratic landslide. Pauline, his youngest daughter, married Nathan Seeley. His mother died. He wrote and published another book, *The Humbugs of the World*, in which he discussed fraudulent lotteries, mediums and mining stocks; the Dutch tulip speculation and the South Sea Bubble; patent medicines and adulterated foods. "But," he wrote, "the greatest humbug of all is the man who believes or pretends to believe that everything and everybody are humbugs." He mounted the platform again and toured the Middle West, lecturing on "Success in Life."

Barnum always declared that he had no superstitions, but he devoted an entire chapter of his autobiography to his constant harassment by the number 13, particularly during this lecture tour. In town after town, hotel clerks assigned him to room 13. Day after day, he noted expenses of exactly $13. Dinner after dinner, he sat 13 at table. Was all this something more than coincidence? He mentioned it in an uneasy letter to a Bridgeport clergyman, who replied cheerily,

> Unbelieving and ungrateful man! What is thirteen but the traditional "baker's dozen," indicating "good measure, pressed down, shaken together and running over"? Insist upon having room No. 13 at every hotel. What do you say respecting the Thirteen Colonies? Was the patriarch Jacob afraid of it when he adopted Ephraim and Manasseh, the two sons of Joseph, so as to complete the magic circle of thirteen? Do you not know that chapter thirteen of First Corinthians is the grandest in the Bible, with verse thirteen as the culmination of all religious thought? And can you read verse thirteen of the fifth chapter of Revelation without the highest rapture?

But Barnum would not be comforted. It was on the thirteenth of July, 1865, he suddenly remembered, that the American Museum had burned to the ground. What did this portend for the new Museum, which had opened on the thirteenth of November? It too burned to the ground, in March 1868, but on the third, not the thirteenth.

That night was bitterly cold. Water from the hoses froze at once. The façade of the building, the signs on the roof, the lampposts in front became "a gorgeous framework of transparent ice." Barnum had recently combined his Museum with the Van Amburgh Menagerie Company, which owned the only giraffe and the smallest African elephant in America. He had hoped to use the menagerie as the nucleus of a public zoo (New York City had none then) and the collection as the nucleus of a national museum. President Andrew Johnson had already authorized government officials in foreign posts to help him collect rarities, and General Grant had contributed one of his campaign hats. The fire destroyed the project. This time, Barnum's losses were shared, but they were still enormous. He had spent $78,000 on alterations and repairs, and he had valued the collection at $288,000, yet his insurance amounted to only $160,000.

Again he was tempted to "accept this fire as a notice to quit and go a-fishing." He yielded to the extent of selling out his interest in Barnum & Van Amburgh, but when George Wood, the proprietor of a smaller Broadway Museum, asked him to join as a consultant, Barnum easily talked himself into it: "Without incurring risk or responsibility, I could occupy portions of my time; my mind would be employed in matters with which I was familiar, and I might gratify my desire to assist in catering to the healthful, wholesome amusement of the rising generation and the public. I should not rust out . . ." Small danger! The years of his greatest achievements were the years ahead.

He entered them slowly, concentrating his energies on East Bridgeport, the town that he still had "on the brain." He contributed ten of his waterfront areas to the new Seaside Park. He drained marshes, laid miles of new streets, planted thousands of shade trees. With all his daughters married and away, Lindencroft became too unwieldy for Charity to handle alone, so he sold it (it was torn down in 1929 and a high school built on its site), and started building again, nearer the seashore, as the doctors recommended for Charity's health.

Meanwhile, he bought a house in New York at 438 Fifth Avenue, on the corner of 39th Street. (A candy store stands there now.) It cost him $80,000. He had his initials on the door; local wits said they stood for "Pull The Bell." Barnum never settled down there. He did a good deal of entertaining, but chiefly he seems to have used the house as a base for various expeditions —to the South, to Niagara, to Cuba, to the Far West. San Francisco refused his offer of $50,000 for the sea lions from Seal Rock, but it could not prevent his carrying off a midget, one Leopold Kahn, whom Barnum promptly re-christened and commissioned, according to his custom, as "Admiral Dot."

Back to Bridgeport from California, the family moved into their new house, Waldemere. Barnum had wanted to call it "Sea-Grove" because the property was thick with fine hickory trees, but his friends protested that such simplicity was unworthy to succeed the

grandiloquence of "Iranistan" and "Lindencroft." Bay-
ard Taylor, the author of Jenny Lind's "Greeting to
America," coined "Waldemere," a condensation of
Wald-am-meer, or Woods-by-the-Sea.

A statue of an Indian about to tomahawk a wolf
startled the visitor at the gate. The grounds were a
mass of shrubs, more statues, flower beds, and bronze
and marble fountains. The house itself, 160 feet long
and topped with a glass dome, was "a pleasant mélange
of Gothic, Italian and French architecture." Colossal
wooden figures flanked the front door to receive hats
and visiting cards. The rooms on the ground floor included the library; the grand salon, containing "all the
elegancies of the present-day millionaire"; the sitting
room, with Jenny Lind's marble Bacchus and the marble of Tom Thumb's foot—both salvaged from the
Iranistan fire; the dining room, with a Sèvres porcelain
service for 200, and the gold and silver services Barnum
had bought in Paris from the estate of Prince Tolen-
shoff. (Barnum tacked a "B" onto the "P. T." and
announced, "This is how I came by my coat-of-arms,
and I daresay many of my neighbors came by theirs in
some such manner too.")

The library, which Barnum called his "workshop"
and sometimes his "growlery," was eight-sided, pan-
eled and furnished in cherry, birch and maple. Around
the walls were portraits of leading journalists and glass
cases of stuffed birds. Barnum's desk stood in an ankle-

deep drift of paper, and gold and silver coins were riveted to the top of his table.

A heavy oak stairway led to the second floor. Three of the guest bedrooms were named for distinguished occupants. The (Horace) Greeley room was done in pale green and white. "Lower tones" were used in the Mark Twain room. No description survives of the Carey room, named for the sister poetesses, Alice and Phoebe Carey; indeed, almost nothing of theirs survives except the hymn of Phoebe's which begins, "One sweetly solemn thought." (Waldemere's guests also included such other literary celebrities as Thackeray, Matthew Arnold and George Augustus Sala, yet none of them printed a word about either the house or its owner.)

An English reporter noted that "The mansion is intersected with a very network of waterpipes, there being scarcely a room that has not its bathroom and lavatory attached." An American reporter noted the elaborate defenses against fire and burglary: alarms on every door and window; a rope from each bedroom to the big bell on the roof; direct telephones to the coachman, the gardener and the police; plus watchdogs, mantraps and hand grenades.

Barnum spent his first night at Waldemere in June, 1869. As usual, he began by prattling about "rural rest," and as usual, he soon found it boring. A few weeks was enough. By midsummer he had organized a world tour for a troupe of midgets headed by General

Tom Thumb and had started them on their way; they would be gone three years. By September he had organized a troupe of his own—himself and nine friends —and had taken them on a buffalo hunt in Kansas. (Barnum was fifty-nine!) He wrote of this experience:

Our ten days' sport afforded me a 'sensation,' but sensations cannot be made to order every day, so in the autumn of 1870, to open a safety-valve for my pent-up energies, I began to prepare a great show enterprise, comprising a Museum, Menagerie, Caravan, Hippodrome, and Circus, of such proportions as to require five hundred men and horses to transport it through the country.

No one was astonished at this relapse from the ideal of "rural rest." Barnum had admitted back in 1868 that the sight of Seal Rock had made his "show fever" begin to rise. The only wonder was that two years would pass before he frankly succumbed to it.

Ups and Downs

BARNUM'S PARTNERS IN THE "GREAT SHOW ENTERPRISE" were two circus veterans: W. C. Coup, an expert manager, and Dan Costello, a famous acrobatic clown. They furnished the brains and the energy; Barnum furnished his name and some of the backing. Their show opened in Brooklyn on April 20, 1871, under three acres of canvas—the largest spread in circus history. The side show offered Admiral Dot ("The Eldorado Elf") and Colonel Goshen ("The Palestine Giant"); the Armless Woman and the Bearded Boy; the Dying Zouave and the Sleeping Beauty—these last, mechanical figures which seemed to breathe. The novelty act was an Italian goat, Alexis, trained to ride a horse bareback and jump through hoops. The feature, or "spec," was "The Crusaders at Acre," with a cast of several hundred. But the main attraction was a family of "wild Fiji Cannibals, ransomed at great cost from the hands of a royal enemy, by whom they were about to be killed and perhaps eaten. I hope soon," Barnum added proudly, "to put them in the way of being converted to Christianity, even if by so doing the title of 'Missionary' be added to the many already given me by the public."

He accompanied the Great Traveling World's Fair, as it was called, on part of its tour, and lectured on temperance in some of the larger cities. His presence was, as always, a drawing card of considerable power, but the bulk of credit for the show's huge success must go to Coup's genius for advertising and transportation. His posters bedecked every barn and fence within 75 miles of the show grounds, and he arranged for excursion trains to bring him customers from every hamlet within poster-shot. As a result, gross receipts for the season reached $400,000.

Coup did not rest there. Since the railroad had so easily brought customers to the show, it might even more easily bring the show to the customers. Next year, accordingly, he took the circus out of wagons and put it into freight cars: 65 of them, with six passenger cars and three locomotives. His overnight jumps broadened from a few miles to 100. He was able to skip the small, miserly towns and pitch his tents only in the wealthier ones; and his season's gross soared to nearly one million dollars.

This 1872 show, the first to move on rails, set still another important precedent; it was the first to offer two rings.

When the tour ended, at Detroit on October 30th, Barnum skimmed off some of the best acts and animals and sent them on a further tour, through the South. The main body, meanwhile, returned to New York, to play the winter season at the Hippotheatron, on Fourteenth Street, which the partners had leased and redecorated at a cost of $60,000. Barnum attended the grand opening; he then joined the Southern tour, and was at breakfast in New Orleans on the morning before Christmas when he received a telegram from his son-in-law in New York:

ABOUT 4 A.M. FIRE DISCOVERED IN BOILER-ROOM OF CIRCUS BUILDING. EVERYTHING DESTROYED EXCEPT 2 ELEPHANTS 1 CAMEL.

S. H. HURD, TREASURER

The fires that consumed Iranistan and two of his museums had taught Barnum no lesson. For the fourth time, his insurance, $90,000, failed to approach his losses, $300,000. But also for the fourth time, his spirit was undaunted. Before even finishing his breakfast, he sent cables ordering rush replacements for all the animals, and wired Hurd:

TELL EDITORS I HAVE CABLED EUROPEAN AGENTS TO
EXPEND HALF MILLION DOLLARS FOR EXTRA ATTRAC-
TIONS. WILL HAVE NEW AND MORE ATTRACTIVE
SHOW THAN EVER EARLY IN APRIL.

And he did. The 1873 show was so elaborate that its
tents covered twice as much ground as ever before, and
its running cost was an unheard-of $5,000 a day. In
September, Barnum put the reins in Coup's able hands
and sailed for Europe to visit the International Exhibition at Vienna, to rest, and to see what he could pick
up for his show. He was ambling through Germany
with an English friend, John Fish, and Fish's young
daughter, Nancy, when Coup wrote that he had leased
the abandoned railroad depot at Madison Avenue and
27th Street, and proposed to remodel it into a gigantic
combination of circus, zoo, aquarium, show ring and
museum. "The Great Roman Hippodrome," he would
call it, but the public would know it as Madison Square
Garden.

Coup's coup was a bold one—too bold for Barnum.
The panic of 1873 had just struck, and he was reluctant
to commit so much capital. He cabled his withdrawal.
Coup cabled back that he didn't need Barnum's money;
the deal was already financed; and Barnum, reassured,
decided to participate after all.

Such seem to be the facts, but they were not gleaned
from Barnum. He was seldom generous with credit to
a rival or even to an associate. Although Coup alone
conceived the Roman Hippodrome and practically

alone brought it to life (he collapsed under the strain), Barnum's autobiography not only minimizes his partner's contribution but ignores his own hesitancy, and grabs the bouquets:

I immediately telegraphed them to take the lease and within 24 hours I was in telegraphic communication with seventeen European cities where I knew were the proper parties to aid me in carrying out a grand and novel enterprise. I visited all the zoological gardens, circuses, and public exhibitions, wherever I went, and thus secured numerous novelties and obtained new and valuable ideas. At Hamburg, I purchased nearly a ship-load of valuable wild animals and rare birds, including elephants, giraffes, a dozen ostriches, etc., etc.

He was still at Hamburg on November 20th when Hurd cabled him that Charity was dead. She was two years older than Barnum and her health had long been declining. The day of her death was almost exactly forty-four years from their wedding day. Streets in Bridgeport preserve the names of Caroline, Helen and Pauline Barnum, and of Barnum himself, and even of Iranistan; but it is for obvious reasons that the street commemorating "the little tailoress" is called not Charity, but Hallett.

Her death wrung from Barnum a cry that "the 'cloud' seemed so utterly black, it was hard to realize it *could* have a silver 'lining.'" He need not have despaired. He found one within a year. In the autumn of 1874, Barnum, aged sixty-four, married Nancy Fish,

twenty-four. All three of his daughters were older than
their stepmother.

Meanwhile, at Coup's request, Barnum resumed his
purchases for the coming season's show. From his English counterparts, the Sanger brothers of Sanger's Circus, he first bought some elephants, camels and horses.
Then he bought sixteen ostriches, ten eland, ten zebra,
a troupe of performing ponies, monkeys, dogs and
goats, and a team of reindeer with Lapland drivers.
Finally he bought duplicates of all the costumes, trap-
pings, and equipment in the Sangers' pageant, "The
Congress of Monarchs." This included "13 gorgeous
carved and gilt emblazoned chariots, harnesses for 162
horses, 1,136 elegant suits of armor, court dresses, etc.;
and a facsimile of all the flags, banners, and everything
else." The bill was just over $200,000.

The menagerie and paraphernalia were shipped
ahead, in time for the opening in mid-April. Barnum
arrived a week later. He went straight to the Hippodrome, and the largest assemblage ever gathered in one
building in New York (about 10,000) applauded as he
drove around the arena in his barouche.

This drive-around was his special vanity. One call
for "Barnum!" and he would summon his carriage and
make the circuit, beaming and bowing. That winter,
King Kalakaua of Hawaii visited the Hippodrome. The
management made much of him; red and blue fireworks spelled out his name; he was given a white rose,
for award to the girl jockey who won a horse race.

Presently the crowd began to chant, "Kalakaua! Barnum! Kalakaua! Barnum!", and at that very moment—by the most *extraordinary* chance—a barouche drove into the arena and up to the box where Kalakaua sat, with Barnum at his side.

Barnum said, "Your Majesty would greatly gratify my countrymen if you would kindly step into this carriage with me and ride around the circle."

The King realized that he was being dragooned into the program as an "Added Attraction! This Night Only!", but he could not refuse without seeming ungracious. He smiled, murmured, "We are all actors," and joined Barnum in the barouche.

The next season, 1875, was a poor one. The nation had not yet recovered from the panic of '73. "Professor" Donaldson, who made a daily balloon ascension from the circus lot, took off from Chicago on July 15 with a reporter from the Chicago *Journal* as passenger, and was never heard of again. Coup's health broke down, and he withdrew; soon he would sell out his interest. Costello had already sold out. Barnum trouped only occasionally. Except for another lecture tour in the autumn, he spent most of the season at Waldemere, entertaining for his young wife with lawn parties, picnics and clambakes, and serving as Mayor of Bridgeport.

He was a good mayor. He closed the saloons on Sundays, he halved the cost of gas-lighting the streets, and he got cheaper and better service from the water works in which he himself was the second largest stockholder. When he retired after his one-year term, the Bridgeport *Leader* declared that he was "far better appreciated for his sterling qualities of rigid independence and honest desire to serve the city than any mayor we have had for years." He refused to run again. He declared he wouldn't do it in return for half of Bridgeport. However, in 1877, he stood for his second term in the Connecticut General Assembly, and was re-elected in 1878.

When the '75 season closed, Barnum, now sixty-five years old and partnerless, took a step daring enough for a syndicate of youngsters: he put his entire show property up at auction—"my Hippodrome and also my 'World's Fair,' consisting of museum, menagerie, and circus property." He wasn't quitting the business: far from it! He was concentrating everything on a traveling circus to take the road in '76, the centennial of the Declaration of Independence.

Naturally, the motif was patriotism. The whole season was one continual Fourth of July. The program promised

> **The Star Spangled Banner**
> **In triumph shall wave**
> **O'er the grandest of shows**
> **Even Barnum e'er gave!**

Each circus day began with a thirteen-gun salute by a battery of cannon, and each performance ended with fireworks depicting Revolutionary scenes. There was a "Father of the Country," a "Goddess of Liberty" and a "Gigantic Live American Eagle." Extras in Continental uniforms marched and countermarched. Every town along the route was requested to ring its bells during the parade, and audiences were invited to join in when the "stupendous" chorus sang "My Country, 'Tis of Thee."

Barnum's next four years were an alternation of calm and confusion, sadness and celebration. He offered the British Government $100,000 for the five-year right to exhibit Cetewayo, the captive King of the Zulus. He spent some time at a ranch he had bought in Colorado. His youngest daughter, Pauline (Mrs. Nathan Seeley), died suddenly, leaving three children, and Barnum wrote Mark Twain, "We have received a terrible blow, but 'God's will be done!' " He traveled to England with his wife and made a lecture tour. He promised $1,000 to any city that would erect a statue to his old adversary, Henry Bergh, President of the Society for the Prevention of Cruelty to Animals, who had finally acknowledged error after a long feud over Barnum's menagerie. He gave Bridgeport thirty more acres for Seaside Park. He corrected, at some length, an English newspaper which had referred to him as "the late Mr. Barnum." He wrote (or at least signed) a book for boys, *The Adventures of Lion Jack*.

Little of all this touched upon the circus. Its interests made few demands upon him during these years.

It seemed to be letting him gather his strength in peace and quiet, while it gathered its own to raise a shout so loud and prolonged that it would clutch his attention and hold it for the rest of his life. No, not a shout, but a trumpet-call and the trumpeter would be elephants. The Elephant Era was about to begin.

17

Barnum and Bailey Join Forces

THE FIRST ELEPHANT THAT AMERICA EVER SAW ARRIVED in New York City on April 13, 1796, and was advertised as possessing

the adroitness of the Beaver, the Intelligence of the Ape, and the Fidelity of the Dog. He is the largest among the Quadrupeds, the earth trembles under his feet; he has the power of tearing up the largest trees and yet is tractable to those who use him well . . . This Elephant is about three years, near six feet high. He is of the largest species, growing to the height of sixteen feet.

The basic components of a circus—its very symbols, emblems and trademarks—are a tent, a clown and an elephant. Barnum had tents and clowns aplenty. He had even some elephants, not to mention a "remarkable anomalous pachyderm named the ELEPHANTUS-

HIPPOPARADOXUS," whatever that was. But he had no baby elephants; especially he had none born in the United States. Neither did anyone else own such a rarity, for the reason that none had been born here since prehistory. And then on March 10, 1880, one *was* born! An elephant cow named Hebe gave birth, in Philadelphia. Wrote Barnum,

The public became wild with excitement. Naturalists and men of science rushed in numbers to examine the wonderful 'little stranger,' and gave glowing reports. Illustrated papers and magazines of this and foreign lands described the baby elephant with pen and pencil.

There was only one shadow on Barnum's rapture: Hebe did not belong to him. She belonged to his strongest competitor, the Great London Circus, Sanger's Royal British Menagerie, and Grand International Allied Shows. This was not three separate circuses, but one, under the joint management of James E. Cooper, James A. Bailey, and James L. Hutchinson. Cooper was soon to die. Of the two other partners, Bailey was the genius, one of the greatest geniuses in circus history.

He was born in Detroit on July 4, 1847. His father and mother died before he reached his teens, so— loathing his brothers and sisters—he ran away and joined a small traveling circus. When one of its advance agents, Frederick H. Bailey, befriended him, the boy discarded his family name, McGinnis, and took his protector's. From then on he repudiated "McGinnis" completely, and once fired a clown (some say a bare-back rider) who bragged that he had played marbles with him when he was Jimmy McGinnis.

He was a spare, silent, nervous man who looked shorter than he actually was. People seeing him for the first time got an impression of a college professor with squint eyes and a big nose. The bottom half of his face was screened by a thick, reddish-gray moustache and beard, and the top half was shadowed by a derby which he seldom took off, for shame of his baldness. When he was worried, he held a silver dollar between his left thumb and ring-finger, and pushed it around with a pencil stub. When he was angry, he chewed rubber bands. He seldom wrote a letter, but he often sent fifty telegrams a day—more on Fridays; he considered Friday lucky and used to postpone important decisions until then.

Organization was Bailey's specialty. His brain was a filing cabinet of timetables, blueprints, maps and inventories. His equestrian director, Fred Bradna, once heard a purchasing agent recommend laying in more horseshoes of a certain type. Bailey told him, "There are sixty-three of them in Bin Three at winter quarters. That's eighteen more than we'll need the rest of the season." The Imperial German Staff sent its Quartermaster General to study Bailey's technique for fast loading, transporting and unloading. He first displayed this ability in his twenties, and he developed it when he and Cooper took their circus on a successful world tour that lasted two years and covered 76,000 miles.

But organization was not the only channel for Bailey's genius. He also understood publicity, as he proved when the baby elephant was born. Barnum wired him, offering $100,000. Bailey not only refused the offer, but reproduced the telegram as an advertisement captioned "What Barnum Thinks of the Baby Elephant."

What Barnum thought of this master stroke is best described by himself:

I had at last met foemen 'worthy of my steel,' and pleased to find comparatively young men with a business talent and energy approximating to my own, I met them in friendly council, and after days of negotiation we decided to join our shows in one mammoth combination.

Did this represent surrender for Barnum? Did he "j'ine 'em" because he couldn't "lick 'em"? Well, look what he got from the deal: the baby elephant, which is what he wanted in the first place; two smart, experienced partners; and his own name at the head of the most unwieldy title on record: "P. T. Barnum's Greatest Show on Earth, Combined with the Great London Circus, Sanger's Royal British Menagerie and Grand International Allied Shows."

Thus began, in 1880, the world-famous partnership of Barnum & Bailey. The two were as different, and as complementary, as pork and beans. Barnum was big and burly. Bailey was slim. Barnum was the "front

man," who gave the interviews, posed for the pictures
and took the bows. Bailey was the silent partner, shy
and retiring; when reporters asked for him, he would
tell them, "Mr. Bailey is not with the show today."
Nothing worried Barnum. Everything worried Bailey—
storms, strangers, superstitions. But despite their dif-
ferences in temperament, each respected the other.
Bailey fully appreciated the pulling power of Barnum's
name; and Barnum used to tell the press, "My partner's got brains—lots of them—and he knows how to
use them. I ought to be jealous of him, and I would if
he weren't my partner."

On one important point the partners were in firmest
agreement: alcohol was a curse. They insisted that their
contracts with all performers contain a temperance
clause. Barnum did so as a moral principle; the practical Bailey, because of the hazard. By now Barnum had
not drunk alcohol in thirty-three years, nor smoked in
twenty, nor ever gambled, except for one flutter in
stock. Unlike most showmen of his (and later) times,
he not only refused to make a percentage arrangement
with grifters, con-men and short-change artists, but
banned them from the lot on penalty of arrest. Whenever a Sunday found him with the circus, he mustered
the employees into the big top and exhorted them to
lead nobler lives. As a result, his circus's direct descend-
ant, the Ringling Brothers and Barnum & Bailey Combined Shows, is known to this day as "The Sunday
School Show."

The new partners' first production opened in New York on March 18,1881, after a torchlight procession witnessed by almost half the population of Manhattan. Music was furnished by a calliope, a chime of bells, a steam organ, a squad of Scottish bagpipers, a choir of Negro jubilee singers, and *four* brass bands—one composed exclusively of American Indians! Small wonder that windows along the route rented for as high as ten dollars!

The performance itself featured Mlle. Zazel, "The Human Projectile," who was hurled forty feet into the arms of an assistant on a trapeze; Captain Costentenus, a Green, "tattooed from head to foot in Chinese Tartary, for rebelling against the King—388 separate designs, over 7,000,000 blood-producing punctures"; General and Mrs. Tom Thumb, back under Barnum's banner; and, of course, the baby elephant, Columbia.

Nine thousand people packed the building on opening night. Three thousand more had to be turned away. One hundred newspaper editors were present as guests of the management; all expenses paid. Inviting them was brilliant publicity. They carried their enthusiasm back home and spread it for miles around, with such effect that when the Big Show went under canvas, a factory in a town along the route posted this notice on circus day: "Closed on account of the greatest interference on earth." There was even a popular song, "Barnum Day":

You must wake and call me early,
   Call me early, mother, dear,
For tomorrow will be the happiest time
   of all the live-long year.
Tomorrow will be the merriest time,
   And we must to town away,
For tomorrow the great show's coming, mother,
   Tomorrow is BARNUM DAY.

Jumbo, the Elephant

BARNUM'S BIGGEST DAY FELL IN 1882, WHEN HE CLOSED a deal for an animal that would become the most famous in the world—so famous that his name would find a place in the English language and would be recognized by Webster's dictionary as meaning (among other things) "huge of its kind." The animal was Jumbo, the largest elephant in captivity.

Jumbo was four years old, the property of some Arab hunters in East Africa, when a Bavarian collector bought him in 1861 and shipped him to the Paris zoo. He was small then, and he had reached nothing like his full size when Paris traded him to the London zoo for a rhinoceros in 1865. Here Jumbo grew apace, in height and fame. But it was not until his height, towering to eleven feet, had attracted Barnum's attention (and a check for $10,000), that his fame towered to the throne itself. For when Jumbo's sale was announced, it is said that Queen Victoria and the Prince of Wales sought ways to buy Barnum off. On February 22, 1882, the London *Daily Telegraph* cabled him:

EDITOR'S COMPLIMENTS. ALL BRITISH CHILDREN DISTRESSED AT ELEPHANT'S DEPARTURE. HUNDREDS OF CORRESPONDENTS BEG US TO INQUIRE ON WHAT TERMS YOU WILL KINDLY RETURN JUMBO. ANSWER, PREPAID, UNLIMITED.

Barnum answered that 51,000,000 Americans were awaiting Jumbo's arrival—£100,000 would not induce him to cancel; and he took advantage of the "prepaid, unlimited" to put in an elaborate advertisement for his new show.

Publication of his cable touched off a demonstration that reverberated up and down Great Britain. Children stormed the zoo for a last, tearful look at the beloved friend whose broad back so many thousands of them had straddled. They choked him with buns and affection, and the gate receipts increased by nearly $2,000 a day. The swollen, doleful crowds perturbed another of the zoo's elephants, a nervous female named Alice. She began to trumpet so mournfully that it unstrung the other animals, and they too began howling, barking, screaming, roaring and moaning.

The American Ambassador, James Russell Lowell, reported home that Jumbo was the only major Anglo-

American problem. Some of its own members sued the Royal Zoological Society for having exceeded its authority. Jumbo cigars, Jumbo fans, Jumbo hats, collars and ties went on sale in London. Menus offered Jumbo soup, Jumbo hash, Jumbo stew, salad and pie. *Punch* printed a long poem by Lord Winchelsea which ended:

> But since in England's fallen state
> She owns two things supremely great,
> Jumbo and Gladstone—(each we find
> The most prodigious of their kind)—
> And one won't budge. Then, Barnum, make
> A fair exchange, for quiet's sake!
> Take the Right Honorable, and go!
> He'll make the better rarer show!
> Leave Jumbo.

Barnum watched from the sidelines, and grinned. Publicity like this was beyond price, beyond creation, beyond control, and more was to come. On Jumbo's day of departure, he lay down at the gate of the zoo and refused to budge. Barnum's agent cabled the news and asked for recommendations. Barnum cabled back, "Let him lie there a week if he wants to! It's the best advertisement in the world!"

Jumbo changed his mind next day and returned to his pen. There he stayed while a crate was built, of thick planks strapped with iron, and mounted on broad wheels. At the same time, the steamship *Assyrian Monarch* was prepared for the biggest passenger that ever left the British shores. Her hatches were widened and

her 'tween-decks deepened. All was ready by the morning of March 25th. Jumbo's keeper, Matthew Scott,
lured him into the crate; the doors were chained shut;
ten horses hauled him to the dock; and presently England's pet was *en route* to America.

He landed at New York on Sunday morning, April
9th. Barnum, Bailey and Hutchinson—all three—were
there to welcome him. Seasickness had cost him half a
ton (he was down to 6½), but otherwise he was in
good health. As the crate was opened, the *Assyrian
Monarch's* first officer, whose appropriate name was
Kidder, remarked to Barnum that Jumbo was fond of
whiskey.

"Oh, no!" Barnum cried. "Don't say that!"

Kidder said, "You don't believe it? I'll prove it to
you," and poured a bottle of whiskey into Jumbo's
maw.

Barnum shouted, "I protest! I protest!", but it was
too late. A newspaper reported that Jumbo "stood mo-
tionless and apparently in rapture." Barnum could only
remark, "Look at the evils of intemperance! Jumbo
would have been twice as large if Scott hadn't stunted
him by giving him a bucket of beer every day." Then,
abruptly switching the subject, he asked Scott, "How
high does he reach up with his trunk? Forty-nine feet,
isn't it?"

Scott said firmly, "Twenty-six feet."

"There's nothing like the truth," said pious Barnum.

Certainly there was nothing—or, at most, very little

—like the truth in the posters he had plastered over New York. The text was standard circus exaggeration:

The Monarch of his Mighty Race
The Universal Synonym for all Stupendous Things
The Gentle and Historic Lord of Beasts
The Prodigious Mountain
The Colossus of the Old and New World

But the illustrations showed Jumbo stretching his trunk to accept a handout from a third-story window (easily forty-nine feet), while a silk-hatted horseman prepared to ride between his vat-like forelegs. Jumbo's actual height at the shoulder was about 11 feet 6 inches. A normal man, afoot and hatless, could not have walked between his forelegs without stooping.

Barnum's exaggerations gave the public no pause at all. Within two weeks after Jumbo landed, he had earned his cost and transportation, a total of about $30,000. Within six weeks, he had earned $336,000. And week by week the huge, mild beast took a stronger hold on the affections of American children.

Three and a half years passed. On September 13, 1885, the circus played St. Thomas, Ontario. The elephants finished their evening act and all thirty-one were loaded aboard their train, except Jumbo and a midget elephant, Tom Thumb. These two were trudging along the track with Matthew Scott when a freight train suddenly rounded a sharp curve close behind. Scott tried to drive his charges into a ditch, but they ran

straight down the track. The locomotive hit Tom
Thumb first, broke his left hind leg and tossed him
aside. But when it struck Jumbo, it stopped dead, then
toppled into the ditch, dragging two cars with it.
Jumbo was knocked to his knees. His skull was frac-
tured, his flanks and feet were gashed, and blood ran
from his mouth. He wrapped his trunk around Scott
and gently drew him down. Death came a few minutes
later.

When his enormous carcass was dissected, a handful
of English coins were found in the stomach—copper,
silver and even gold. Barnum gave the skeleton to the
American Museum of Natural History, in New York.
The hide, which weighed 1,538 pounds, he mounted on
a hardwood frame and gave to the Barnum Museum
of Natural History at Tufts College, of which he was a
trustee. (The Tufts emblem is Jumbo's head.) Both
skeleton and hide Barnum later borrowed back, for display with the nervous Alice, whom he had bought and
was advertising as "Jumbo's widow," but he eventually
returned them to their respective museums, and they are
there now. The midget elephant recovered from his in-
jury, but walked with a limp until his death. *His* hide
is in the Barnum Museum at Bridgeport.

One final note: There is a certain grisly aptness in
the fact that the fatal locomotive belonged to the Grand
Trunk Railway.

Showman to the End

THE YEAR BEFORE JUMBO'S DEATH, BARNUM'S AGENTS
had bought another elephant, unique like Jumbo and
like him destined for a tragic end. This was Toung
Taloung, the first "Sacred White Elephant" of Burma
ever to go on public display. Exporting these beasts
was considered blasphemous, so Toung Taloung's pur-
chase in Rangoon and passage to New York had to be
negotiated secretly, delicately and expensively.

White elephants are not a pure, milky white; except
for a few pinkish patches, they can hardly be distinguished from ordinary elephants. Two years earlier, in
1882, a rival showman whitewashed an ordinary elephant, exhibited it briefly, and then declared that it
had suddenly died. Barnum wasn't deceived. He said,
"It was simply *un*-dyed!" But he had not expected his

genuine white elephant to look so commonplace. He was frankly disappointed. So was the public. Although he pulled out every stop on his publicity organ and printed acres of handbills, and tapestried half the barns in America with gaudy posters, he never really cared for his rare prize. Nor was there such mourning as there had been for Jumbo, when Toung Taloung was burned to death on November 20, 1887.

The circus had just gone into its new winter quarters at Bridgeport. The fire broke out in the menagerie building at 10 P.M. and spread so rapidly that the only animals saved were thirty elephants and one lion. Toung Taloung's keeper led him to safety again and again, but he broke free each time and rushed back into the flames. "Jumbo's widow," the nervous Alice, was another of the four elephants lost. A third was Gracie, who lumbered away alone and was found next morning swimming in icy Long Island Sound. She died of exposure and exhaustion as she was being towed ashore.

The last part of the building to crash down was an end wall painted with a heroic portrait of Barnum. For minutes his face, framed in fire, hung against the black curtain of the night. Then there was the terrifying rumor that some boa constrictors had escaped and were slithering around the neighborhood—in the darkness and confusion, someone had mistaken the writhing fire hoses. To cap everything, there was the incident of Nimrod, a tame lion. His keeper led him out by the mane, quite calmly, only to have a panicky onlooker shoot at him. Frightened, Nimrod bolted into a barn, where he attacked a cow and calf. Their owner, the Widow Gilligan, heard their cries, grabbed a broom, and began drubbing what she took—in the dim light— for a big stray dog.

"Shoo!" she shouted. "Shoo, dog!"

The "dog" kept eating, and the widow kept drubbing, and presently some circus employees arrived. When they told Mrs. Gilligan what the "dog" was, she fainted.

The loss on this, Barnum's fifth, fire was huge as before: $250,000. And, as before, his insurance was paltry: $31,000. But, as before, there was one important consolation: every human life was spared.

Barnum was seventy-seven now, and the ranks around him were thinning every year. His first wife was dead. Their daughter Pauline was dead. Jenny Lind had died a few days before the last fire. Barnum's family aside, the death that affected him most deeply was little Charlie Stratton's, on July 15, 1883. They had been devoted associates for more than forty years. Barnum once estimated that his various attractions had sold a grand total of 82,464,000 tickets, and that 20,400,000 of them, or nearly a quarter, were to see Tom Thumb. The famous little man was forty-five years old, and forty inches high, and weighed seventy pounds, when apoplexy struck him down. He was a Thirty-Second Degree Mason and a Knight Templar. so he was buried with Masonic honors, in Mountain Grove

Cemetery at Bridgeport, which Barnum had helped create. Ten thousand people attended the service.

Back in 1857, Charlie had commissioned a life-size statue of himself, in granite. This was now mounted on a forty-foot marble shaft (ironically, the tallest in the cemetery), and the midget's stone eyes at last could see over the heads of his fellow men. The shaft cracked in the course of time, and the statue was remounted on a lower pedestal, but there is no danger that Charlie's fame will become correspondingly smaller. As "Jumbo" is still a synonym for hugeness (Jumbo asparagus, Jumbo sandwich and, contradictorily, Jumbo shrimp), so "Tom Thumb" represents tininess throughout the English language. There is a Tom Thumb rosebush that a teacup will cover, and every miniature golf course in the land is a memorial to Charlie Stratton.

He once wrote a clergyman who had asked for his autograph,

I read the Bible every day and am very fond of reading the New Testament. I adore my Creator and know that He is good to us all. He has given me a small body but I believe that He has not contracted my heart, nor brain, nor soul. I shall praise His name evermore.

Charlie was a good little man on the whole, but he had one vice: he was a spendthrift. Although he earned millions in his youth, his wild extravagance in later years reduced his estate to a scant $16,000, plus some real estate. His widow, Lavinia, had to sell her own property and return to show business. Her new troupe included two Italian midgets, Count Primo Magri and his brother, Baron Ernesto Magri. The Baron could whistle like a flute. The Count could fence and box, and play the piano and the piccolo. He and Lavinia were married less than two years after her first husband's death, and they lived together happily until her own death in 1919, aged 78. Despite Charlie's squandering, Lavinia never ceased to love him. She always wore a gold locket with his picture in it, and she was buried beside him, under a stone marked with the one word, WIFE.

So many deaths in so few years sorrowed and slowed Barnum. He withdrew from active management of the circus and contented himself with serving as a sort of living advertisement for "The Greatest Show on Earth"—and, of course, for his own renown. It was huge by now. "Barnum" and "circus" were synonymous. Like Jumbo and Tom Thumb, Barnum had become a figure of speech in his lifetime. Webster's dictionary paid him the honor of recognizing "Barnumism" and "Barnumize" as aspects of "bombastic display." He even achieved the rank of a semi-myth. At a circus performance in Toronto in the '80's, he heard a youngster ask his father, "Which cage is Barnum in?" At another performance, in Erie, Pennsylvania, he eavesdropped on an elderly farm couple sitting in front of him.

"Barnum himself," he heard the old man say. "That's

the one thing I'd give more to see than the whole show: Barnum himself!"

Presently four bare-back horses galloped into the center ring, with a handsome young rider turning somersaults from one to another. That did it. The old farmer jumped up and shouted, "I'll bet five dollars it's Barnum! There ain't another man in America who can do that but Barnum!"

Barnum did not set him straight.

The peak of his fame loomed in 1889, when Bailey arranged to ship the show to London at the end of its American tour. It was the biggest show in circus history. The spectacle, "Nero, or the Burning of Rome," had a cast of 1,900. Even so, Barnum was the main attraction. England had forgiven and forgotten his abduction of Jumbo. She regarded him no longer as a pirate or humbug or braggart, but as a dear, jolly old boy. Street urchins called "Good old Barnum!" when he drove past. Madame Tussaud put his image on display in her famous wax works. Two hundred peers, politicians and journalists gave him a testimonial banquet. England's premier actor, Sir Henry Irving, gave him another, at which his voice was recorded.[1] But his

---

[1] This recording was reissued in 1940 with an introduction by Professor William Lyon Phelps, of Yale, who called Barnum "The greatest circus man who ever lived . . . the greatest psychologist who ever lived . . . the Shakespeare of advertising." Barnum's voice is clear and firm, and his accent is a surprising combination of Boston and Brooklyn—i.e., he uses the broad A, but says *hoid* for *heard, woild* for *world;* he also says *hoppy* for *happy, thon* for *than.*

greatest tribute was paid twice daily, at the matinée and evening performances, when his carriage rolled into the arena to a surf of cheers, and stopped for him to doff his silk hat and announce, "I suppose you all come to see Barnum. Wa-al, I'm Barnum!"

The Prince of Wales[2] greeted him warmly: "We are old friends and need no introduction." The Princess of Wales came four times. Barnum asked their son, Prince George,[3] if he was staying to the end of the program. The Prince told him, "I shall remain here until they sing 'God Save Grandmother'!"

Three ocean liners brought the show back to America in the spring of 1890, and Barnum retired to rest at his new home, Marina. The house was new, but the site was not. Marina was built only thirty-odd inches from Waldemere, which was then split into three houses, the three hauled away to different locations (where they all are still in use today), and the cellar filled in and turfed over. Barnum let it be known that Waldemere had become too large and expensive for a family now consisting of only himself and his wife, but it is possible that Nancy felt Charity's shadow on Waldemere and wanted a house of her own.

Barnum devoted the early summer to bringing his autobiography up to date, and to publishing a new book, *Dollars and Sense, or How to Get On, The Whole Secret in a Nutshell.* On July 4, the day before

[2] Later King Edward VII.
[3] Later King George V.

his eightieth birthday, he gave an afternoon party for his children, grandchildren and great-grandchildren, and that evening he gave one for all his employees and their families. He spent August at a hotel in the Adirondacks. The owner, his old friend Paul Smith, prided himself on serving only the finest of everything. When Barnum complained that the "so-called" pepper was "at least one-half peas," Smith dictated a furious letter to the grocer, who replied meekly that even the purest pepper *had* to be one-half P's.

No doubt Barnum was still chuckling over his "score" when, in November, he was stricken with brain fever. The attack soon passed. He resumed discussions of next season's show with Bailey, he gave a parsonage to a Bridgeport church at Thanksgiving, and he contributed to every local charity at Christmas. But his full strength never returned; he would never leave Marina again.

The new year saw the beginning of his long, slow, final decline. At first, he did not recognize it as such. Nancy Barnum, knowing how carefully he read the daily papers, requested them not even to hint at his failing health, and the editors kept considerate silence. But early in April, Barnum himself realized that the end was near. He did not quail. Calmly, he set his affairs in order and gave instructions for his funeral. Death came early in the evening of April 7, 1891. It was kind to him, his widow wrote, "and no physical pain disturbed the quiet figure on the little bed. With un-

daunted heart and unclouded brain, there passed one
of the most remarkable and best loved men of his
country." His last words were a request to know the
Big Show's receipts that afternoon at Madison Square
Garden.

All Bridgeport went into mourning. On the day of his
funeral, flags flew at half mast. Public and private
buildings were hung with black. Shop windows displayed his portrait, black-draped and flower-wreathed.
He was buried in Mountain Grove Cemetery beneath
a simple stone, not far from his "little but sympathizing friend," Tom Thumb.

His estate amounted to $4,100,000. Charities would
get much of it, but $40,000 a year was set aside for
his young widow. Nancy Barnum lived on at Marina
until the turn of the century, then moved to Paris, re-
married twice, and died in 1927, aged seventy-seven.
Marina is now part of the University of Bridgeport,
whose campus sweeps down to Long Island Sound, past
a statue of Barnum given to the city by his former
partners, Bailey, Hutchinson and Cole. Bailey died
(from an insect bite) in 1906, Hutchinson in 1910,
Cole in 1915. Next year the circus consolidated with its
chief rival and has operated ever since as the Ringling
Brothers and Barnum & Bailey Combined Shows.

The news of Barnum's death flashed around the
world. The *Times* of London commented:

> His name is a proverb already, and a proverb it
> will continue until mankind has ceased to find

pleasure in the comedy of the showman and his patrons—the comedy of the harmless deceiver and the willingly deceived.

Jokesmiths immediately set about developing the comedy of Barnum in Heaven:

> St. Peter: "What's all that noise inside, Gabriel?"
>
> Gabriel: "They're laughing at Barnum and Noah. Noah's mad because Barnum disparaged his show."

And:

> St. Peter (to Barnum at the Gate): "Can't come in, sir!"
>
> Barnum: "What! No chance for me?"
>
> St. Peter: "No, sir; you had your show on earth."

Barnum himself never doubted his welcome. When he sailed home from England for the last time, the Bishop of London told him, "Good-bye, Mr. Barnum! I shall meet you in Heaven, I hope."

Barnum said confidently, "You will if you're there!"

INDEX

LANDMARK BOOKS

LANDMARK BOOKS *continued*

WORLD LANDMARK BOOKS